THE

Bhagavad Gita

OR

The Message of the Master

Compiled and adapted from numerous
old and new translations of the
Original Sanscrit Text

By YOGI RAMACHARAKA

REVISED EDITION

THE YOGI PUBLICATION SOCIETY

CHICAGO, ILL., U. S. A.

Printed by
YOGA PUBLICATION SOCIETY

ISBN #0-911662-10-3

CONTENTS.

INTRODUCTION.

The *"Bhagavad Gita,"* sometimes called *"The Lord's Lay,"* or the *"Message of the Master,"* is an episode of the great Hindu epic, the *Mahabharata,* in the *Sixth* (or *"Bhishma"*) *Parva.* It enjoys the highest esteem among the Hindu people, and is constantly quoted there as a great authority regarding doctrine. Its philosophy embodies the prevailing Hindu beliefs, as expounded by the Brahmans, and in its teachings it subtly blends into a harmonious whole the varying points of doctrine of *Patanjali, Kapila* and of the *Vedas.* It is supposed to have been written by *Vyasa* whose personality is veiled in doubt for of the time of his existence in the world no record seems to have been kept.

To the reader who finds in this marvelous dialogue merely the record of a literal conversation dressed up in fancy by the Oriental imagination, the real beauty and purpose of the teaching is lost. But to him who is able

to pierce the outer covering, which surrounds
all of the great Oriental writings, and find
beyond that the esoteric teachings, this poem
is one of the grandest that has ever been
given the race.   One must needs read behind
the covering—and between the lines, in order
to understand the *Bhagavad Gita*.   No attempt has been made by the compiler of this
publication to interpret the inner teachings of
the *Gita*.   It has, as the Hindu teachers instruct their pupils, seven texts, each super-
imposed upon the other, so that each man
may read his own lesson from it, according to
his plane of unfoldment.   Each will get from
it that which is fitted to his stage of unfoldment.   And each reading will bring to light
new beauties, for the mind of the reader will
grow with each perusal and soon be prepared
for the understanding of higher phases of
thought.

There have been a number of English
translations of the *Gita*, from the first effort
of Charles Wilkins, in India, in 1785, up to
the present time.   Some are very good, others
indifferent, and others actually misleading
and causing confusion.   Some of these trans-

lations have evidently been made by persons inclining to certain schools of philosophy; and the meaning, as colored by their own philosophical glasses, while most satisfactory to them and their followers, is distracting to those outside the pale, who have had the opportunity of comparing the various editions.

This particular edition, issued by us, is not a new translation, but rather a compilation from the best of the various good translations of Hindu and English translators, some of which are now out of print, or inaccessible to the general public. The compiler has endeavored to give the *spirit* of the teachings, in a plain, practical, understandable form, adapted to the requirements and needs of the English speaking reader, although such a presentation has often necessitated the sacrifice of any attempt at literary merit. In fact this book makes no claim whatsoever to literary style. It merely seeks to carry the Message contained within its pages, in plain words and simple form, to those who are ready for it.

The compiler has purposely omitted many Sanscrit terms which have proved to be confusing to the English reader, notably the many titles and names bestowed upon both *Krishna*, and *Arjuna*, in the original. In some editions the English reader is confused by these, and has often been led to imagine that there were several persons engaged in conversation instead of but two principal characters. We trust that we have simplified the text, and that those who read it will understand the reason for the plain, simple, and unpolished style adopted.

To those who, after studying this little book, are desirous of further acquainting themselves with the subject—and who seek the Inner Doctrine underlying the various forms of the Hindu Philosophy, we would recommend the Lessons in *"Gnani Yoga,"* issued by our house. These Lessons contain, in the plainest form and style, the higher teachings of the Yogi Philosophy—the Inner Doctrines.

We further recommend to the readers of this work a little book, also issued by us, bearing the title of *"The Spirit of the Upanishads,"* which contains a collection of texts, quotations and selections from the great sacred books of India. The texts, etc., bear directly upon the subjects touched upon in the *Bhagavad Gita,* and will aid the student in obtaining a fuller conception of the underlying principles of the teachings.

We strongly advise that those who intend to read this book, should first read the little notice, which follows this formal prefatory introduction. By so doing, the reader will become acquainted with certain circumstances concerning the characters, scene, and theme of the story, which will make the reading of the text far more pleasing and instructive.

We trust that this little book may fulfill its mission in the carrying abroad the *"Message of the Master."*

THE YOGI PUBLICATION SOCIETY.

Chicago, Ill.

THE SCENE; THEME; AND CHARACTERS.

The scene of the action, or story, is laid in the low, level land in India, between the *Jumna* and the *Sarsooti* rivers—now known as *Kurnul* and *Jheed*—the land being known in the story as "the plain of the *Kurus*." The word *"Kuru"* was the name of the common ancestor of the contending factions in the battle—the theme of the story—the opposing factions being known, respectively, as the *"Kurus,"* and the *"Pandus,"* as you will notice a little farther on.

The theme of the great Hindu epic, the *Mahabharata*, of which the *Bhagavad Gita* is an episode, is the great war which was carried on between two factions, or parties, of a certain large tribe, or family, the descendants of the common ancestor *Kuru*. The bone of contention between the opposing factions was the sovereignty of *Hastinapura*, which some authorities suppose to be identical with modern *Delhi*. The elder branch, faction, or party, bore the general name of the whole people—*Kurus*: the younger branch bearing the name of *Pandus*, the term being derived from the name of *Pandu*, the father of the five chiefs commanding the army of their faction or branch.

The whole *Kuru* people were an old family, many generations having passed between the time of *Kuru*, its founder, and the time of the battle between the two branches. It is stated that the family, or people, originally inhabited a region beyond the Himalayas, and afterward emigrated into the northwest of the peninsula, and there founded the nucleus of a race who called themselves the *Arya*, or exalted, the term being intended to distinguish them from the lower tribes whom they conquered, and whose territory they wrested from them and occupied.

The history of the people immediately preceding the great war, and from the occurrences of which the war itself arose, is as follows:

At the capital of the country, a city called *Hastinapura* (supposed to be modern *Delhi*), reigned the king *Vichitravirya*. He married two sisters, but he died shortly after the dual-marriage, leaving no children. Following the custom of the ancient Oriental peoples, and moved by love and respect for his deceased brother, his half-brother, the *Vyasa*, married the widows, and begat two sons named *Dhritarashtra* and *Pandu*. The eldest son, *Dhritarashtra*, had one hundred sons, the eldest being named *Duryodhana*. The younger brother, *Pandu*, had five sons, all great warriors, and known as the "five *Pandu* princes." *Dhritarashtra* became blind, and, although remaining nominally king, his real power passed to his eldest son *Duryodhana*, who influenced his father and caused him to banish from the land his cousins, the five *Pandu* princes.

After many vicissitudes, travels, and hardships, these princes returned to their native land, surrounded by their friends and sympathizers, and reinforced by warriors furnished by neighboring friendly kings, the whole forming a mighty army. They marched on to the plain of the *Kurus*, and began a campaign against the older branch of the family, the partisans and followers of

Dhritarashtra, who gathered under the leadership of the eldest son of the latter, named *Duryodhana,* who was in command by reason of his father's blindness; and under the general name of the family, *"the Kurus"* the elder branch began a determined resistance to the invasion or attack of the younger branch, the *Pandus.*

This brings us to the scene and time of the battle. The *Kuru* faction led by *Duryodhana* (acting for his blind father, *Dhritarashtra*) was arrayed on one side; and on the other side was the hosts of the *Pandus,* led by the five *Pandu* princes. The active command of the *Kuru* army was vested in *Bhishma,* the oldest war-chief of his faction; the *Pandu* army being led by *Bhima,* a renowned warrior. ARJUNA, one of the five *Pandu* princes, and one of the leading characters in the story, was present at the battle with his brothers, and was accompanied in his war chariot by the human incarnation of THE SUPREME SPIRIT—KRISHNA, the latter having become the friend and companion of ARJUNA as a reward for the fortitude with which the latter had borne his persecutions, and as a recognition for the nobility of character displayed by him.

The battle was opened by *Bhishma*, the *Kuru* chieftain, blowing his great war-shell or conch, to the sound of which his followers joined with the blare of their battle shells and horns. ARJUNA, and the *Pandu* host answer the challenge with mighty blasts. The fight then begins with great flights of arrows, in which both sides exert themselves to the utmost. ARJUNA, at the beginning of the battle, asks KRISHNA to drive his chariot to a position where he may witness the two contending parties. From the desired position ARJUNA surveys the two battle lines, and is overcome with horror at the sight of blood relatives and friends opposing each other in the two contending armies. He sees dear ones on both sides, seeking each other's blood. He is overcome with the thought of the horror of the fratricidal war, and, throwing down his weapons, he declares that he would rather die without defending himself, than be the cause of the death of his kinsmen on the other side. KRISHNA replies with subtle philosophical discourse, which forms the greater part of the episode of the epic, called the *Bhagavad Gita,* the poem or story which is offered to your consideration in this little book. ARJUNA is made to see the weakness of his position, judged from the absolute point-of-view, and he consents to play his part in the drama. The battle finally results in the overthrow of the *Kurus,* or elder branch, and the triumph of the *Pandus,* or younger branch, the latter being ARJUNA's party.

The scene opens at a place removed from the battle field, where the old blind king *Dhritarashtra* inquires of the faithful *Sanjaya,* of the events transpiring at the front. *Sanjaya* replies, giving the news of the day, his story comprising the poem.

The battle, of course, serves but as a setting for the discourse of KRISHNA to ARJUNA, at least so far as this poem is concerned.

The Bhagavad Gita

PART I.

THE GLOOM OF ARJUNA.

Spoke DHRITARASHTRA, King of the Kurus, to SANJAYA, the faithful, saying :

"Tell me, O *Sanjaya*, of my people and the *Pandus*, assembled in battle array on the plain of the *Kurus*! What have they been doing?"

SANJAYA: "Thy son *Duryodhana*, commander of thy hosts of battle, when he beheld the host of the *Pandus*, arrayed for strife and combat, approached his preceptor, *Drona*, the son of *Bharadvaja*, saying:

"Behold, O Master, the mighty host of the sons of *Pandu*, comprising the vast array of experienced and bold fighting-men, commanded by thy former pupil, the wily and resourceful son of *Drupada*.

"Behold how, gathered together in the opposing ranks are mighty warriors in their chariots of battle. Their names are synonyms for valor, strength and cunning.

" 'And on our own side, gathered together, under my command, are the greatest warriors of our people, heroes, valiant and experienced, each well armed with his favorite weapons, and most ready to use them; and all devoted to me and my cause and willing and anxious to risk and renounce their lives for my sake.

" 'But, alas, O Master, this army of ours, although most valiant and though commanded by *Bhishma*, seems unto me too insufficient and weak, while the enemy, commanded by *Bhima*, and confronting us in threatening array, seems more strong and sufficient. Therefore, let all the captains of my host prepare to stand by *Bhishma*, to support and guard him well.'

"Then *Bhishma*, the ancient chief of the *Kurus*, blew his great battle-shell, sounding it like unto the roar of the lion, to awaken the spirits and courage of the *Kurus*. And answering its great roar, there sounded at once innumerable other shells and horns, drums and tabors; and other instruments of warlike music, so that the sound was tumultuous and stirred the hearts of the *Kurus* to valiant deeds and high resolves.

"Then, in brave response and mighty defiance, sounded forth the instruments of the hosts of the *Pandus*.

"Standing in their great war-chariots, trimmed with gold and precious stones, and drawn by milk-white steeds, *Krishna*, the incarnation of God, and *Arjuna*, the son of *Pandu*, sounded their war shells until the air quivered in vibration. And all the rest of the mighty host of the *Pandus* joined in the defiance, and the mightiest warriors of the throng sounded their instruments again and again, until the sound was as the sound of the violent thunder, and earth's surface answered in responsive rhythm. And the hosts of the *Kurus* were affrighted and dismayed.

"Then Arjuna, perceiving that the hosts of Kuru stood ready to begin the fight, and seeing that even then the arrows were beginning to wing their flight through the air, raising his bow, spake thus to *Krishna*, the God, who stood beside him in the chariot:"

"O *Krishna*, drive thou, I pray thee, my chariot so that it stand between the two op-

posing armies, that I may gaze upon the men
of the *Kuru* hosts that stand ready to begin
this bloody fight, and with whom I must combat, battle, and strive in this fray. Let me
look upon mine enemies, the followers of the
evil-minded and vindictive commander of the
Kurus!"

Then drove *Krishna* the chariot containing
himself and *Arjuna*, until at last it stood in a
space between the two opposing hosts. And
then *Krishna* bade *Arjuna* look attentively
upon the hostile army of the *Kurus*, and then
upon the faces of his friends, the host of the
Pandus. And *Arjuna*, looking, saw arrayed
on either side, grandsires, uncles, cousins,
tutors, sons and brothers. Gazing farther he
saw, likewise, near relations and bosom
friends. Loved ones, benefactors, playmates,
companions, and many others whose welfare
was dear to him, he saw standing opposed to
him, fretting for the fight. And also standing
back of him, awaiting the word to join him in
the fray, stood others of like relationship,
both of blood and of friendship.

And *Arjuna*, seeing these things, was overcome with gloom. Compassion, pity, com-

punction, despondency, and sadness filled his
heart, and, sighing deeply, with sorrow permeating
his tones, he spake thus to *Krishna*,
who stood by his side in the chariot:

"O *Krishna* now that I behold the faces
and forms of my kindred and loved ones, thus
arrayed against each other, and chafing for
the fight, my heart faileth me. My legs
tremble; mine arms refuse to do my bidding;
my face is drawn in agony; my skin burns as
with a fever; my hair standeth upon end; my
brain reels; my whole body is convulsed with
horror; my war-bow slips from my fingers.

"Evil omens fill the air, and strange voices
seem to speak around me, so that I am overcome
with confusion and indecision. What
good can come from my killing these my kindred,
and loved ones, and friends? I desire
not the glory of victory, O *Krishna*. Nor do
I long for the kingdoms or dominion; nor do
I seek for enjoyments of life, or pleasure; nor
even life itself. These things appear most
vain and undesirable to me when those for
whom they were to be coveted have abandoned
life and all else.

"Tutors, sons and fathers; grandsires and

grandsons; uncles and nephews; cousins, kindred all; and friends, comrades and companions, stand before me, inviting my arrows. Even though these may desire to kill me; nay, may even actually slay me—still do I wish not to slay them, even though the three great regions of the universe be my reward, much less the petty thing we call the earth, or the pettier kingdoms thereof.

"Were I to kill my relatives, the sons of *Dhritarashtra*, what happiness or pleasure could be ours, O great one. Should we destroy them, remorse would be our companion and indweller. Therefore, it seems to me as a truth that we should refrain from slaying these, our kinsmen, for how can we be happy, hereafter, if we are guilty of having destroyed those of our race.

"It is no excuse for us, who see these things as we do, to say that these others have minds so depraved and bloodthirsty that they can see no evil in the shedding of the blood of their kinsmen and friends. Can such an excuse justify us, who knoweth better, in committing a like horror?

"We have been taught that in the annihilation of a family, the ancient virtue of the family is destroyed. And in the destruction of the virtue and traditions of a people, vice and impiety overwhelm the whole race. Thus may the women of the family become corrupt, and the purity of the blood vanish. This adulteration of the blood prevents the performance of the ceremonies of the rites due the ancestors, according to our ancient customs, and the forefathers, if the teachings of the people be true, must sink into a state of misery and unhappiness.

"Thus by the crimes of those who destroy their own relations, sore contamination of the family-virtue and glory is made possible, and the forefathers of the race are given great mortification, and pain and degradation, as we have been taught from childhood, as a people, O *Krishna*.

"O woe is me! Woe unto us who are preparing to commit the horrible crime of murdering these, our blood-relations and kind, for the bauble of dominion—the lust of power!

"Rather would I bare my breast to the weapons of the *Kurus*, and let them drink deep of the blood of my heart—rather would

I await their coming, unresistingly, and unarmed meet their thrusts—than commit this foul crime against my blood-relations. Surely, that for me would be far the better! O woe is me, and woe unto us all!"

And having spoken thus, *Arjuna* sank back upon the seat of his chariot, and sitting down, he put away from him his bow and his arrows, and, placing his head between his hands, he gave away to the gloom, despondency and grief that was consuming his heart.

THUS ENDETH PART I OF THE BHAGAVAD GITA, WHICH PART IS CALLED "THE GLOOM OF ARJUNA."

PART II.

Krishna, the Blessed One, filled with love, compassion and pity for *Arjuna* who was thus smitten with compunction and gloom, and whose eyes were overflowing with tears of grief, spake unto him these words:

"Whence cometh this dejection, O *Arjuna*, which hath overcometh thee who art standing on the field of battle. This folly and unmanly weakness **is** most disgraceful, contrary to thy duty—such weakeneth the foundation of honor. Yield not thyself to this unmanly weakness, for it ill fitteth thee who hath been called the Tormentor Of His Foes. Shake off this despicable fancy, and stand up bravely and resolutely, O Conqueror of Foes!"

ARJUNA: "Alas O *Krishna*, how can I attack with the arrows of the battle, such worthy and honorable men as *Bhishma* and *Drona*—they who are full worthy of my reverence, O Master—how shall I do this wicked thing?

"Better were it for me to eat even the dry and tasteless crust of the ragged beggar, than to be the instrument of death to these most noble and worshipful men, who were my preceptors and teachers! Were I to slay these well-wishers of mine, verily I should partake of but blood-besprinkled possessions, wealth and pleasures—a horrid feast to which the beggar's crust would be noble and most worthy.

"I cannot see whether it would be better for me whether we be the victors or the defeated, for I should not wish to live after having caused the death of those arrayed against us—my kinsmen and friends—the sons and people of *Kuru's* king *Dhritarashtra,* who now confront us in angry battle array. My compassion weighs down my heart even unto faintness, and my mind reels confusedly before the problem presented to it. What is Right Action for me—what is my Duty? O most blessed *Krishna*, my Lord, decide these weighty questions for me—tell me what is Right. I, Thy disciple and student, beg for Thy instruction in this my hour of dire need.

"So confused and dazed am I, that my

understanding is confounded by the dictates of my Duty, and I can discover nothing that will give peace to the fever of mind which burneth within me, and drieth up my faculties. Even though I should gain a kingdom on earth, surpassing all other earthly kingdoms, even as the sun surpasseth the stars— nay, even though I were to gain dominion over the Hosts of Heaven, my grief would not be assuaged."

"Nay, nay, I will not fight—I will not fight."

And, saying these words *Arjuna* became silent. But *Krishna,* smiling most tenderly upon the despondent prince, standing, cast down in mind, in the midst of the two armies, spake unto him these words:

"Thou grievest for those who need not thy grief, *Arjuna,* yet thy words are not those of the foolish, but bear within them the seeds of wisdom. Thy utterances have a wise sound, but yet express only the outer wisdom, and fail to show the flower of the inner doctrine of the wise. They are true, and yet not wholly true—the half-truth is apparent—but the missing half is the deeper portion.

"The truly wise grieve neither for the dead, nor yet for the living. Just as the brave man feareth neither Death nor Life, so doth the wise man avoid grief over either, though the half-wise grieve over either or both, according to mood and circumstance.

"Know thou, O Prince of *Pandu*, that there never was a time when I, nor thou, nor any of these princes of earth *was not;* nor shall there ever come a time, hereafter, when any of us shall *cease to be*.

"As the soul, wearing this material body, experienceth the stages of infancy, youth, manhood, and old age, even so shall it, in due time, pass on to another body, and in other incarnations shall it again live, and move and play its part. Those who have attained the wisdom of the Inner Doctrine, know these things, and fail to be moved by aught that cometh to pass in this world of change; to such Life and Death are but words, and both are but surface aspects of the deeper Being.

"The senses, through their appropriate faculties of the mind, give thee reports of cold and heat, pleasure and pain. But these changes come and go; they are shifting, transient and inconstant. Bear them with equanimity, bravely and patiently, O Prince.

"For, verily I say unto you, that the man whom these things have ceased to further torment—he who stands steadfast, undisturbed by pleasure and pain—he to whom all things seem alike—such an one, say I, hath acquired the road to Immortality.

"That which is unreal hath no shadow of Real Being, notwithstanding the illusion of appearance and false knowledge. And that which hath Real Being hath never ceased to be—*can never cease to be*, in spite of all appearances to the contrary. The wise have inquired into these things, O *Arjuna,* and have discovered the real Essence, and Inner Meaning of things.

"Know that The Absolute, which pervades all things, is indestructible. No one can work the destruction of the Imperishable One.

"These bodies, which act as enveloping coverings for the souls occupying them, are but finite things of the moment—and not the Real Man at all. They perish as all finite things perish. Let them perish. Up, O

Prince of Pandu, knowing these things, prepare to fight!

"He who in his ignorance thinketh: 'I slay,' or 'I am slain,' babbleth like an infant lacking knowledge. Of a truth, none can slay—none can be slain.

"Take unto thy inner mind, this truth, O Prince! Verily, the Real Man—the Spirit of Man—is neither born, nor doth it die. Unborn, undying, ancient, perpetual and eternal, it hath endured and will endure forever. The body may die; be slain; be destroyed completely; but He that hath occupied it remaineth unharmed.

"How can a man who knoweth the truth —that the Real Man is eternal, indestructible, superior to time, change and accident, commit the folly of thinking that he can either kill; cause to be killed; or be killed himself?

"As a man throweth away his old garments, replacing them with new and brighter ones, even so the Dweller of the body, having quitted its old mortal frame, entereth into others which are new and freshly prepared for it.

"Weapons pierce and cut not the Real Man, nor doth the fire burn him; the water affecteth him not, nor doth the wind dry him nor blow him away. For he is impregnable and impervious to these things of the world of change; he is eternal, permanent, unchangeable and unalterable; He is Real.

"In his Essence he is immutable, unthinkable, inconceivable, unknowable; therefore, why shouldst thou allow thyself to be made a weakling by childish grief?

"Or if, perchance, thou believeth not these things, and liveth in the illusion of belief in birth and death as realities—even so, asketh thee, why shouldst thou lament and grieve? For, if this last be true, then as certain as it is that all men have been born, so is it certain that all men must die; therefore why grieve and fret thyself over the inevitable and unavoidable?

"To those who lack the Inner Wisdom, there is no knowledge of whence we come, or whither we go; such know only what is at the moment. Why should they, then disturb themselves regarding this thing or that—why should they lament?

"Some wonder greatly regarding the soul, while others hear of and speak of it with in-

credulity and lack of comprehension. And
no one, by mortal mind, really understandeth
the mystery, nor knoweth it in its true and
essential nature, in spite of all that has been
said, taught and thought, concerning it.

"This Real Man that inhabiteth the body,
O *Arjuna,* is invulnerable to harm, hurt, or
death—therefore, why shouldst thou trouble
thyself further about the matter? Instead,
it is far more worthy of thee, thou Prince of
the Warrior Caste, to face thy Duty in the
matter, manfully and resolutely. The Duty
of a soldier is to fight—and fight well. And
the reward of Duty well done is the opening
of the heaven of thy kind, which is possible
only to warriors who are so fortunate as to be
able to participate in a glorious, just and
righteous battle, coming to them unsought.

"And shouldest thou decline the battle, and
cast away thy righteous Duty with thy weapons, surely thou wouldst commit a grave
crime against thine honor, thy duty and thy
people. And, men will see it only as such,
and will recite thy crimes in terms of perpetual
dishonor; and to such as thou, O Prince, the
pangs of death are preferable to the reproach

of such dishonor. The generals of the host will think thou hast fled from the field from a sense of cowardly fear; those who have thought so highly of thee until now, will hold thee in abhorrence and contempt. Even thine enemies will speak of thee in shameful terms, with many a jest and sneer at thy lack of strength and courage; and what could be more painful than that, to such as thou art?

"If thou chance to be slain in the battle, the warrior's heaven wilt be thy reward; if victorious thou emergeth from the fray, the joys of earth await thee. Therefore, O Prince of Pandu, arise and fight! being willing to take whatever betideth thee—be it pain or pleasure; loss or gain; victory or defeat; thine only concern being whether thou hast done thy best —prepare thou for the fray. That is your plain Duty!

"Know thou, O Arjuna, that in these words of mine hath been set before thine understanding the Doctrine, which deals with the speculative philosophy of life and things. Now, prepare thyself for the teachings of the other school; thou shalt there find escape from the bonds of action, and be forever after free from them.

"In this there is no loss or waste of effort, nor is there therein any danger of transgression, as even a small portion of this knowledge and practice delivereth one from great fear and danger, because in this branch of knowledge there is but a single object, upon which the mind may safely concentrate.

"Many are they, who, saturating themselves with the letter of the spiritual writings and teachings, and failing to catch the true spirit thereof, take great delight in technical controversies regarding the text. Hair-splitting definitions and abstruse interpretations are the pleasures and amusements of such men. Such are tainted with worldly lusts, and, therefore, incline toward a belief in a heaven filled with objects and employments in accordance with their desires and tastes, instead of the final spiritual goal of all great souls. Flowery words, and imposing ceremonies are invented by these people, and, among them, there is much talk of rewards for this observance, and punishment for that lack of it. To these whose minds incline to such teachings, the use of the concentrated, determined reason and the still higher Spiritual Consciousness, is unknown.

"The object of the spiritual teachings is the instruction of the thoughtful ones to the end that they may rise above these Three Qualities or Gunas. Be thou free from them, O *Arjuna!* Free thyself from the pairs of opposites—the changeful things of finite life; and careless about the same dwelleth thou in the consciousness of the Real Self. Be free from worldly anxiety, and the fierce cravings for material possessions. Be self-centered and uncontrolled by the illusions of the finite world.

"Just as does the full water-tank, when drawn upon, supply the crystal fluid which will fill every vessel according to its shape and size, so do the spiritual teachings, when drawn upon, furnish just what is needed to fill the mind of the earnest student, according to the degree and character of its development.

"So rule thy actions and thought that thy motive be Right Doing rather than the Reward which may come from the action. Be not moved by hope or expectation of what may come as the result of thy action. But also must thou avoid the temptation of Inaction, which cometh often to him who has lost the illusion of the hope of reward for action.

"Stand thou between these two extremes, O Prince, and perform thy Duty because it is Duty, freeing thyself from all desire of reward for the performance, and concerning not thyself whether the consequences seem good or evil; success or failure. Do thy best, according to the dictates of thy Duty, and then maintain that equal-mindedness which is the mark of the Yogi.

"Important though Right Action be, yet it yields precedence to Right Thinking. Therefore take thou refuge in the peace and calm of Right Thinking, O *Arjuna*, for they who stake their well-being upon action alone must needs lose happiness and peace, and find themselves possessed only of misery and discontent.

"He who hath attained the Yogi consciousness is able to rise above good and evil results. Strive to attain unto this consciousness; for it is the key to the mystery of action.

"Those who have so far attained that they mentally relinquish the possible fruit of the Right Action, are on the road to the mastery of Karma. Their chains, which bind them to the round of involuntary rebirth, become loosened, and in the end drop from their limbs and leave them free. Eternal bliss is in sight for these.

"When thou shalt rise beyond the plane of illusion, then shalt thou cease to disturb thyself regarding doctrines, theology, disputations concerning rites or ceremonies, and other useless trimmings upon the cloth of spiritual thought. Then shalt thou be liberated from attachments to sacred books, to writings of learned theologians, or to those who would interpret that which they fail themselves to understand; but instead, shalt thou fix thy mind in earnest contemplation of the Spirit, and thus reach the harmony with thy Real Self, which underlies all."

ARJUNA: "Tell me, O *Krishna,* thou whose knowledge includes all wisdom—tell me, I pray, the distinguishing characteristics of the Wise Man, who, stable of mind, blessed with spiritual knowledge, and fixed in contemplation, is worthy of the name of Sage. How sitteth, moveth, or acteth he? How may he be known to ordinary men?"

KRISHNA: "Know, O Prince, that when a man freeth himself from the bonds of the desires of his heart, and findeth satisfaction in the Real Self within himself—such a one has attained Spiritual Consciousness. His mind is disturbed neither by adversity nor by prosperity; accepting both, he is tied to neither. Anger, fear and worry have been cast off by him as discarded garments. He is worthy of the name of Sage.

"Such a man meets the charges and events of life, be they favorable or unfavorable, with equanimity—likes and dislikes being foreign to him, for he is no longer bound by attachments, or things.

"When a man hath attained true spiritual knowledge, he becometh like unto the tortoise which is able to draw within its shell its limbs, for such a man may withdraw his faculties of sense-impression from the objects of sense, and shelter them from the illusions of the sense-world, well protected by the armor of the Spirit.

"It is true that there are those who are able to refrain from gratification of the senses, but the desire for gratification still disturbs. But he who has found the Real Self within and who knoweth what he hath found—even Desire fadeth away from such a one, and temptation is temptation no more, but becomes even as a shadow which hath been effaced by the glare of the noon-sun overhead.

"The abstainer is oft carried away by a sudden rush of tumultuous desire, which sweeps away his resolutions—but he who knoweth the Real Self to be the only Reality is master of himself, his desires and his senses. Wrapt in contemplation of the Real, the unreal exists not for him.

"The man who allows his mind to dwell closely on the objects of sense, becomes so wrapped up in the object of his contemplation that he creates an attachment which binds him to them. From this attachment ariseth Desire; from Desire springeth Passion; from Passion come Folly and Recklessness; from these proceed loss of Memory; and from loss of Memory cometh loss of Reason; thus he loseth all.

"But he who hath gained freedom from attachm : to, or fear of, objects of sense; he who findeth his strength and love in the

Real Self; he gaineth Peace. And in that
Peace which passeth all understanding, he
finds release from all the troubles and pains of
life. And, his mind, now freed from these
disturbing elements, is open to the inflow of
Wisdom and Knowledge.

"There is no true Knowledge possible for
those who have not entered into this Peace,
for without the Peace there can be no calm,
and without calm how can there be knowledge or Wisdom? Outside of the Peace there
is naught but the storm of the sense-desires,
which sweepeth away the faculties of knowledge, as the fierce gale sweepeth away the
mighty ship which is borne on the bosom of
the ocean.

"Verily, only he, O Prince, whose senses are
shielded from the object of sense, by the pro-
tection of the knowledge of the Spirit—only
he is possessed of wisdom.

"To him, what seemeth the bright things of
day to the mass, are known to be the things
of darkness and ignorance—and what seemeth
dark as night to the many, he seeth suffused
with the light of noonday. That is to say, O
Prince, that that which seemeth real to the

men of the sense-world, is known to be illusion by the Sage. And that which seemeth unreal and non-existent to the crowd, is known to the Sage as the only Reality. Such is the difference in the powers and vision of men.

"The man whose heart is like unto the ocean, into which all rivers flow, but remaineth constant and unmoved in its bed—the man, who feeleth the inrush of the desires, passions and inclinations, but who is moved not thereby, hath obtained Peace. But he who lusteth in his lust is without Peace, and is forever the plaything of disturbing desires.

He who hath divorced himself from the effects of desires and abandoned the lusts of the flesh, in thought as in action, walketh straight to Peace. He, who hath left behind him Pride, Vain-glory, and Selfishness, goeth straight to Happiness. Yea, so goeth he!

"This, O Prince of Pandu, is the state of Union with the Real Self—the Blissful state—the state of Spiritual Consciousness. And he who hath attained it no longer is bewildered nor led astray by Illusion. If having attained it, he dwelleth therein unto the hour of death,

he passeth straight to the Bosom of the
Father."

THUS ENDETH PART II OF THE BHAGAVAD
GITA, WHICH PART IS CALLED "THE INNER
DOCTRINE."

PART III.

THE SECRET OF WORK.

Then spake *Arjuna,* the Pandu Prince, unto *Krishna,* the Blessed Lord, saying:

"O Bestower of Knowledge! If, as thou hath said unto me, Right Thinking is more important than Right Action—if the Thought be superior to the Deed—then wherefore dost thou incite me to Action? Why dost thou urge me on to this horrible battle with my kinsmen and friends? Thy subtle words and doubtful speech confuse my understanding, and the remembrance thereof causeth my brain to spin and whirl unsteadily. Inform me, I pray thee —and inform me with certainty—of the one course that leads toward Peace and Satisfaction."

KRISHNA: "As I have already told thee, O Pandu Prince, there are two roads to the goal thou seeketh. The first of these is the road of Right Thought; and the second that of Right Action. Each road hath its travelers, who declare their own road to be the only true one

And, yet, I say unto thee, that both of these roads are one, when seen from above. Listen to my words!

"He is deceived who thinketh that by shrinking from action, and resting in inactivity, he escapeth the results of action. Nor doth he gain happiness from such practices. There is no such thing as real inaction, for all the Universe is in constant activity, and no single point in the Universe may escape the general law.

"No one—not even for a moment—can remain inactive. For the laws of his nature impel him to constant activity of body, or mind, or both. Even against his will, is he impelled into action of some kind. There is no escape from the universal law.

"And, again, I say unto you, that he, who restrains and controls his sense-organs and instruments of activity, and, yet, in his foolish mind, dwells upon the objects and things of the senses, is a deluded and deceived soul.

"But he, who, expressing his mind in Right Action, through Duty, without attachment to rewards, performeth his work in the world—verily, he is to be esteemed wise and worthy.

"Act well thy part in the world—perform

well thine allotted tasks—take hold of that work which lies nearest thy hand, and do it the best that is in thy power to do—and it will be well with thee. Work is far preferable to idleness—the one doth strengthen the mind and body, and is conducive to a long and normal life; while the other doth weaken both body and mind, and leadeth to an impotent and unhappy life, of uncertain duration.

"The race of men is bound because of action performed from motives of reward and gain; it hath become attached to its desired objects, and must toil on, bound, until freedom comes at last. But do thou avoid, this folly, O *Arjuna,* and do thou perform thy dutiful and proper tasks unattached and free. Perform thy tasks for the sake of Duty to the Real Self alone, and for no other motive.

Rememberest thou, Adjuna, the ancient teachings which inform thee of the creation of the world, and of the words the Creator spake to his created beings? Listen to his words, which I repeat to thee: 'Worship! Sacrifice! And remember the Source Of All Things—the Bestower of Desired Objects! Think of the gods, that the gods may think of you! Ask that ye may receive! He who receiveth the gifts of the gods, and faileth to accord to them his thought and recognition is like unto a thief. From food, creatures are nourished and grown; from rain cometh the food; from the gods come the rain in response to the desires and demands of man; and the desires and demands of man are forms of action; and the actions proceed from the One—All-pervading Life.'

"He, who, living in this world of action, attempts to refrain from action—he, who, enjoying the fruits of action of the acting world, would still shirk from his share of the work and action of the world—he who would thus idle away his life lives a life most vain and shameful. He who profiteth by the turn of the wheel, at every moment of his life, yet refuseth to touch his hand to it to impart motion, is a shirker of tasks and a thief who takes, giving nothing in return.

"But wise is he who acteth otherwise, and who performeth well his work of the world, providing, that he be unattached to the fruits thereof and that he be always centered in the knowledge of the Real Self. For such an one

,oncerneth not himself regarding what is be‑
ing done in the world, nor what is being left
undone; in all created things, there is no one
thing upon which he needs lean, or in which
he need place dependence for his being. Par‑
taking of all, and acting in all—according to
the dictates of Duty—he never depends upon
any external thing; his trust, and hope and
knowledge are fixed upon the Imperishable—
the only sure dependence.

"Therefore, such action, springing from
Duty, free from attachment or dependence,
leadeth one straight to the consciousness and
plane of Spirit.

"Rememberest thou not, that *Janaka* and
many others reached a stage of perfection by
means of Good Works and Right Action?
Thou shouldst take note of the universal prac‑
tice of mankind, and act accordingly, for such
universal practice must needs be the result
of long experience in happiness. The wise, in
all times, have taught the virtue of work and
action, and thou mayst well follow the best of
thy race.

"Considereth thou Me, O Prince! Thou
knowest that there is nothing in the Universe

of Universes which I desire, or which is
necessary for Me to perform. Nor is it pos-
sible for anything to be attained by Me, which
I have not already attained. And yet, O
Pandu Prince, and yet, I am in constant
action and motion. I work without ceasing.
And if I were not constantly in action, O
Arjuna, would not men follow my example?
Should I refrain from action, would these
Universes not fall into ruin, and utter confu-
sion and chaos reign?

"Remember, O Arjuna, that even as the
undeveloped do labor and act through attachment and hope of reward, so should the developed and enlightened act and work for the
common cause and universal law, and not
from attachment to personal ends and objects.

"It is not wisdom to unsettle the minds of
the undeveloped with these thoughts; let
them labor on, each doing the best that he
can; but do thou and the other wise ones,
work in harmony with me and endeavor to
render all action attractive to them. And
this is best done by the force of example.

"Place the responsibility for action upon
the shoulders of Him to whom it belongs—the

One; and then doeth thy duty as a man should, with mind fixed on the Real Self, and without expectation of reward. The fool, in his conceit, saith 'I do this,' and 'I did that,' but the wise look behind the personality for the cause and effect of action.

Knowing the whole truth, thou shouldst beware of unsettling the minds of those not yet prepared to grasp it, as untimely teaching may drive from their work such as seee only half-truths, and become unsettled thereby.

"Then, prepare to fight, Arjuna, throwing the responsibility where it belongs, and with thy mind freed from egotism and selfish expectation, but centered upon the Real Self, engage in the battle task before thee!

"Those who with confidence and faith shall constantly follow this teaching shall be made free even by works and action. But those who reject the teachings of Truth and act contrary thereto shall suffer the fate of the senseless and deluded ones and be confused and lacking in Peace.

"But the wise man also seeketh that which is in harmony with his own nature and endeavors to fit his life according thereto, rather than to seek after things contrary to his nature. Let each do the best he can, in his own way, and in accordance with the highest within his own character.

"Beware of the fixed aversion or affection, for objects of sense which each will find within himself. They are obstacles on the path, and the wise beware of putting themselves in the power of these enemies within their camp.

"And, finally, O Arjuna, remember this, that it is better to do one's own duty, humble and insignificant though it be, than to seek to perform the duty of another, no matter how much nobler that may seem. Better death in the performance of one's own duty and tasks, than victor in performing the borrowed duty of another. The assumed tasks are full of danger. Doeth the task at hand. When you are prepared to perform a higher one, it will be placed before you, in the same manner."

ARJUNA: "But, O *Krishna*, it oft would seem that a man is pushed into evil doing, by some power outside of himself—as if, contrary to his inclinations, he were impelled by some secret force. Inform me, thou, of this mystery."

KRISHNA: "It is the essence of his accumulated Desires, combining for attack, that urgeth him on. It is this enemy of man, called lust or passion, begotten of the carnal nature, full of sin and error. As the flame is dimmed by the smoke, the bright metal by the rust, so is the understanding of man obscured by this foe called Desire, which rageth like the fire, and is difficult of being extinguished. The senses and the mind are its seat; and through these it serves to confound and confuse the Discrimination. Thy first task should be to conquer this foul dweller in the mind. Mastering first the senses, and sense organs, proceedeth thou then to put to death this thing of evil.

"The senses are great and powerful; but greater and more powerful than the Senses is the Mind; and greater than the Mind is the Will; and greater than the Will is the Real Self.

"So, thus, recognizing the Real Self as higher than all, proceedeth thou to govern the Personal Self, by the power of the Real Self, and thus conquer this foul monster, Desire, most difficult to seize, and yet possible of being mastered by the Real Self. Then bind him fast for evermore, thy slave instead of thy master."

THUS ENDETH PART III OF THE BHAGAVAD GITA, WHICH PART IS CALLED "THE SECRET OF WORK."

PART IV.

SPIRITUAL KNOWLEDGE.

And the Blessed Lord spake further unto *Arjuna,* the Pandu Prince, as together they stood in the war chariot between the two armies, saying:

"This eternal teaching of Yoga, spake I unto *Vivaswat,* whom men call the Sun—the Lord of Light. And he in turn communicated it to *Manu,* the reigning spirit. And he in turn transmitted it to *Ikshwaku,* the founder of the solar dynasty. And from him it was passed on from higher to lower degree, until it was known to the Royal-Sages.

"But, know, O Prince, that as the years have passed by, this noble teaching hath decayed and its light hath grown dim. Almost lost hath become its inner spirit, and men know naught but its letter. Such is ever the fate of Truth among the race of men.

"But once more, to thee, do I declare the Truth, knowing that thou art a true devotee.

Listen well to it, *Arjuna,* because it is the supreme mystery and ancient Truth."

ARJUNA: "How mayeth I solve the riddle, O Krishna, when thou sayest that thou taught this truth to *Vivaswat* in the beginning—for it is taught that *Vivaswat* existed before Time began, and thou wert born in more recent time?"

KRISHNAS "Many have been my births and re-births, O Prince—and many also have been thine own. But between us lies this difference —I am conscious of all my lives, but thou lackest remembrance of thine.

"Listen to this great secret. Although I am above birth and rebirth, or Law, being the Lord of all there is, for all emanateth from me—still do I will to appear in my own universe, and am therefore born by my own Power and Thought, and Will.

"Knoweth thou this, O Prince, that whenever the world declineth in virtue and righteousness; and vice and injustice mount the throne—then cometh I, the Lord, and revisit my world in visible form, and mingleth as a man with men, and by my influence and teachings do I destroy the evil and injustice, and reestablish virtue and righteousness. Many times have I thus appeared; many times hereafter shall I come again.

"He who is able to pierce my disguise, and who knoweth me in my Essence, when he quitteth his mortal frame, is released from rebirth in worlds, but is granted the joy of dwelling with Me.

"Many, freeing themselves from anger, hate, fear and attachment to things, and keeping their minds fixed upon me, have been purified by the Sacred Flame of Wisdom, and have come to dwell with Me.

"No matter by what path men approach Me, they are made welcome. For all paths no matter how diverse lead straight to Me. All paths are mine, notwithstanding by what names they may be called.

"Even they who tread the path of the lower deities and imaginary gods and who pray to them for success through action— even these, say I, meet with reward, for they reap the success that comes from earnest application and industrious action. Through the laws of Mind and Nature, do their gods, real or imagined, answer them.

"But I am the creator of all mankind in all of its phases and forms. From me proceed the four castes, with their distinguishing qualities and activities. Know me as the creator of all these, though in Myself I am changeless and without qualities.

"In my essence I am free from the effects of action; and I have not any desire for rewards or the fruits of actions; for these things are produced by My power and have no hold upon Me. Verily I say that he who is able to see and perceive Me as I am, in mine own essence—he is freed from the effects of action. Understanding this, the Wise Men of old still performed actions, but were not attached to the fruits thereof, and so moved on to Deliverance. Follow thou their example and reap their reward.

"But even the wise, at times, have been confused as to what was Action and what Inaction. Therefore, I will inform thee regarding this. I shalt tell thee of what action consisteth, knowing which thou shalt be relieved from evil and set free.

"He who would learn the truth concerning action must grasp these three things—Action,

Inaction, and Wrong Action. Difficult to clearly discern is the path of Action.

"He who hath so far attained that he is able to see Action in Inaction and Inaction in Action is among the wise of his race, and to him cometh harmony and peace even while he performeth actions. His works are free from the bonds of desire, and his activities are purged of their dross by the Flame of Wisdom.

"Having freed himself from attachment to the fruits of actions, and not being dependent thereon, he is enjoying Inaction even while in the very exercise of Action. Freed from all and dependent upon naught, his mind and senses under control, he goeth through the motion of action and seemeth even to perform it in the most approved and successful manner; but full well he knoweth that his Real Self is not entangled in the action, and is far above reward or punishment, for victory or defeat. He is released from the consequences of Action, which are bonds and chains holding down those who know not the truth.

"Being content with what the day bring-

eth forth; and being freed from like and dislike; being without envy; being willing to accept success or failure with a cheerful heart,
after having done his best, he is not bound.
For him who hath killed attachment and who
dwelleth harmoniously with his mind fixed in
the true knowledge and wisdom, all the binding effects of action melt away as the cloud
before the rising sun.

"As the sacrifice which goeth to the Eternal
One is in reality but a mere form of That to
which it goes—so he who knoweth Me in all
of his actions shall come to Me.

"Some there be who offer up sacrifices to
the lesser gods, and others there be who worship the Divine Principle in the fire; others
pour their sense-desires upon the altar; others
offer up the very functions of life; others still
there be who make offering of the sacrifice of
wealth—or who practice austerity as a token
of worship—or who meditate in silence and
thought; others there be who practice Yoga
as a worship; and some make vows and render devotional exercises; still others practice
sacred breathings as their share of offering;
others perform fastings.

"All make sacrifices, though their offerings be far different in nature and kind. And all are benefitted by the spirit which causes their form of sacrifice; all gain merit by the sacrificial spirit behind the observance. There is much virtue and merit in self-restraint and self-mastery, O Prince, and thus do the sacrificers come nearer to Me. Yea, they who rise from their sacrificese with increased spiritual comprehension draw nearer unto Me. But, for him who maketh no sacrifices, O Prince, there is no merit for him in this world —how then can there be merit for him in another?

"Thou hast seen that there are many forms of sacrifices and worship in the world, O Arjuna. Knoweth thou, then, that Action pervadeth all these forms. Knowing this, thou art freed from error. But better than the sacrifice of objects and things, O Prince, is the offering of Wisdom. Wisdom, in itself, is the sum of all Action—the Spiritual Knowing comprehends all Action.

"Learn thou this lesson by study, thought, service and investigation. The Wise Ones— the Seers—the possessors of the Inner Knowledge—will aid thee, from time to time, as thou art ready. When the pupil is ready, the Master appeareth. When thou most needeth knowledge—the next link in thy chain—wait in patience and confidence, for lo! suddenly at thy hand, shalt come that which thou needest. And having acquired this wisdom, O Prince, thou shalt be freed from confusion, misunderstanding and error; for by means of this Wisdom shalt thou know all beings as in the One Life, and thus in Me.

"Though thou hath been the greatest of sinners, yet even thou shalt be carried over the sea of error upon the boat of Truth. As the flame reduceth the wood to ashes which are borne away by the wind, so shalt the fire of Truth convert into ashes the result of the evil actions which thou hast committed in ignorance and error. Verily, in the world, there is no purifying agent like unto the Flame of Spiritual Truth. And he who acquireth it findeth himself purged of the dross of Personality and in time findeth the Real Self.

"He that hath great faith, that mastereth the Personal Self and its sense-attachments— hath attained Wisdom, and is on the path to the Supreme Peace. But the ignorant and those of little faith, find not even the beginning of the path. Without faith there is no happiness or peace, neither in this world nor the next.

"Free from the bonds of action is that man who by means of Spiritual Knowledge hath attached himself to Wisdom and thus torn asunder the illusion of doubt—he indeed is Free.

"Then rise in thy might, O Arjuna, Prince of the Pandus, seize thy bright and gleaming sword of Spiritual Wisdom, and cut thou, with one strong sweep of thy blade, the bonds of doubt and unbelief which confine thy mind and heart. Arise, O Prince, and perform thine appointed action!"

THUS ENDETH PART IV, OF THE BHAGVAD GITA, WHICH PART IS CALLED "SPIRITUAL KNOWLEDGE."

PART V.

Then, again, spake *Arjuna,* the Pandu Prince, unto *Krishna,* the Blessed Lord, saying:

"O *Krishna,* thou speakest in paradoxes, for first dost thou praise renunciation of actions, and then praisest thou the performance of service through actions. Pray which of these two hath the greater merit? And I beg of thee that thou telleth me plainly and without danger of further doubt and confusion on my part."

KRISHNA: "Say I unto thee, O Prince, that both Renunciation of Action and Service through Action have great merit—both lead toward the highest goal. But, verily, I say unto thee, that, of the two, the performance of Service is preferable to the Renunciation of Action—Right Action is better than is Inaction. But even in the use of these terms, thou must be watchful lest thou fail into confusion. For truly is he the greatest

Renouncer who neither seeks action nor yet avoids it—who neither runs after action, nor yet runs away from it. He thus renounceth all, both likes and dislikes. Free from the pairs of opposites is he, and calm and content, ready to perform all tasks and actions that may be set before him, and yet likewise ready to refrain from all action, not being attached thereto; yea, verily is such a one freed from bondage.

"The grown-up children who are entering into the study of the Truth are most prone to speak of Renunciation of Action and the Performance of Right Action as different. Sages know them both as one. Both lead to the same goal, and the followers of the one attain that which is attained by the followers of the other. He who seeth beneath the surface of things, perceiveth that in their essence both are one.

"But it is a most difficult task to attain to Renunciation of Action without the performance of Service through Action, O Arjuna, and the man who harmonizes the two ways is blessed indeed, for he is well started upon the road to Peace. He who is engaged in the performance of Right Action, and who at the same time keepeth himself free from the desire of the fruit of action—he thus renounceth action, although performing it. He is thus able to subdue his senses and desires, and by such mastery is enabled to see beyond the Personal Self, and to become conscious of the Real Self which is one with the Real Self of all beings. He knoweth the Universal Life, and that from which the Universal Life proceeds. And so knowing and acting, he is not bound by the bonds of Action, but is free therefrom.

"Being so, he is at harmony between the two ideas. And, although he seeth, heareth, feeleth, smelleth, eateth, moveth, sleepeth, breatheth, yet knoweth he that the Real Self underlieth all action and therefore may say 'Of my Personal Self, do I nothing.' Truly he may also say 'The senses perform their parts in the sense-world.—let them play— I am not bound by, nor deceived by them, for I know them for what they are.'

"He, who thus acteth, seeing back of all action the Real Self which is actionless, is free from the stain of the world. He remaineth like the lotus-leaf which is harmed not by the waters around it. The wise, having abandoned attachment, perform the actions of body, mind and intellect and even of the senses understandingly, and ever have Right Action and Purification in view. Harmonized, and abandoning the desire and hope of reward for actions, they gain Peace. But those who lack this harmony and who are held fast in the bonds of desire of rewards for actions are troubled and filled with unrest and dissatisfaction.

"The wise man, setting himself free, mentally, from actions and their results, dwelleth in the Temple of the Spirit, even that which men call the Body, resting calmly therein, at peace, and neither desiring to act, nor causing to act, and yet always willing to play well his part in action when Duty calleth him. For he knoweth that although his body, senses, and mind may engage in action, yet the Real Self remaineth forever undisturbed. For the Real Self acteth not in these ways—such belong to the lower nature of man, through the qualities of such nature. The Real Self performeth neither good nor evil actions; it remaineth above these distinctions and their manifestations.

"The Light of Wisdom is oft obscured by the Smoke of Ignorance; and man is deluded thereby, and seeth the smoke for the flame, knowing not what lieth behind the smoke. But, they, who are able to pierce behind the pall of smoke, perceive the bright Flame of the Spirit, shining like unto an infinity of suns, free and undimmed by the smoke which hath shielded it from the eyes of the majority of men.

"Meditating upon the Real Self—blended into the Real Self—seated firmly in the knowledge of the Real Self—loving with fierce devotion the Real Self—the wise are freed from their bonds. Their eyes are cleared from the smoke which filleth the eyes of men, blinding them; and they pass into those higher states, from which none return to these lower planes of existence. Blessed beyond measure are such.

"He whose eyes have been freed from the smoke of error and illusion, looks with equal feeling and respect upon the revered, learned and enlightened leader of men and the veriest outcast among men. For, know you, Arjuna, that the eyes so freed from illusion see the Personalities of forms of life as so unreal when compared with the Real Self, that even very great worldly distinctions disappear when viewed from such a height. Those whose minds are able to dwell in this realiza tion, gain the Life above Illusion even in this life, for in this realization is the realization of the Real Self.

"Verily those who see the Real Self ever underlying all that seems to be—the only Reality in the world of apparent Reality—who see this and are able to dwell in that knowledge, even as the wood floateth upon the bosom of the waters—they refrain from over-joy on obtaining that which is pleasant; and from over-sorrow on receiving that which is unpleasant. They have freed themselves from attachment to these pairs of opposites—these fruits of action and external objects; and therefore they find inexpressible joy in the knowledge and consciousness of the Real Self. And, having entered into this Real Consciousness they pass into the realm of Eternal Bliss and Peace.

"For know thou, Arjuna, that the joys and pleasures of the senses—those so-called satis-factions that arise from external objects—are verily the wombs of future pain. They belong to the world of beginnings and endings—and the wise man taketh no delight in such. He who, even in this world of senses and sense-objects, is so filled with the strength which proceedeth from true knowledge, that he is able to bear with equanimity the urgings and longings of the desire nature—and who, thus bearing them, is able to hold them in their places with master hand—he hath gained harmony, and is indeed thrice-blessed.

"He who hath found the Peace Within, and who hath been so illumined that he findeth his joy and happiness within himself—and knoweth that within him is the Kingdom of Heaven—verily, he gaineth the Peace of the Real Self, because he hath blended himself with the Real Self. They, from whom the il-lusion of duality and separation hath been removed, see all Life as One, and emanating from One. The welfare of the All becomes the welfare of the One to them; and to such cometh the Peace of the One. This Peace which passeth all Understanding, cometh to those who know themselves for what they are, rather than for what they seem to the smoke-blinded eyes of the world. Being freed from the bondage of desire and sense-passion they master their thoughts by their Wisdom—and theire senses by their thoughts.

"Having mastered the body by the Yogi teachings, so that the same is rendered a fit habitation for the soul, and keeping it well swept and in good order, under the eye of the mind—having senses, faculties, mind and understanding well controlled and in good condition—with the eye of the soul forever fixed upon Freedom and Attainment of Peace—the Sage casteth behind him the wornout sheaths of desire, fear, passion and lust, and passeth into the state of Freedom and attainment. Knowing Me for what I am—knowing that I rejoice in the Mastery of Self-Control—knowing that I am the Lord of the Universe, and the true lover of all souls —the Wise One findeth and knoweth Me in my Peace, at the last."

THUS ENDETH PART V, OF THE BHAGVAD GITA, WHICH PART IS CALLED "RENUNCIATION."

To the heart that is serene whatever happens to us is right

PART VI.

Then spake, again, *Krishna,* the Blessed Lord, unto *Arjuna,* the Prince of the Pandus, saying:

"Hearken unto my words, O Prince. Truly say I unto thee, that he, who performeth honorably and to the best of his ability, such Action as may appear to him to be plain and righteous Duty, remembering always that he has naught to do with the reward or fruits of the Action, is both a Renouncer of Action, and also a Performer of the Service of Right Action. More truly is he an Ascetic and Renouncer than he who merely refuses to perform Actions; for the one hath the spirit of the doctrine, while the other hath grasped merely the empty shell of form and letter. Know thou such Intelligent Right Action as Renunciation; and also know that the best of Right Action without Intelligent understanding of the renunciation of results is not Right Action at all.

70

"In the earlier stages of the path, Right Action is taught as the most merit-gaining plan; while to the same man, when he hath attained Wisdom and Understanding of the Doctrine, and hath also freed himself from attachment even unto Right Action, then to him Calm Meditation and Serene Peace of Mind is called the better. To each is given, according to his needs and stage of unfoldment. When a man frees himself from attachment to the Fruits of Action; Action itself; or the objects of the sense-world—then hath he reached the highest stage of Right Action.

"Let each raise up his soul by the knowledge of the Real Self. And let not the soul be depressed nor cast down, for truly hath it been said that the Real Self is the lover of the soul, and its true friend, notwithstanding the fact that the ignorant soul may feel that the Real Self is its enemy, inasmuch as it tends to annihilate its sense of separate personality.

"The Real Self is the friend of him in whom the Personality hath yielded mastery; but to him whose personality is defiant, the Real Self appeareth as his bitterest foe. Whereas,

in truth, the Real Self is seeking but to liber-
ate the soul from its own bondage of illusion
and error—seeking to add to its riches, rather
than to rob and despoil it of things of worth.
Thus, through the smoke of illusion and error, the True Friend is seen as the Bitter
Enemy.

"The soul of him who hath perceived the
Real Self within him is peaceful and calm, in
heat and cold, in pleasure and pain, in that
which the world calleth honor and dishonor.
The wise man is content with the knowledge
and wisdom which hath been unfolded to him,
as earth's rarest treasures.   His senses are
harmonized by Self-Mastery, and Wisdom
hath taken the place of Desire.

"Such an one excelleth in wisdom, to such
an extent that he regardeth both friends and
enemies, aliens and countrymen, saints and
sinners, the righteous and unrighteous—with
equal love and sense of brotherhood.

"The Yogi sitteth in his secret place, engaged in meditation and deep thought.   With
mind and body mastered by the Real Self, he
is divorced from greed and desire of reward.
He sitteth in a clean place, neither too high or

too low; his seat made of a cloth, a black antelope skin, and *kusha* grass, arranged as his teachers have well taught him, in accordance with the traditions of his kind. Sitting thus, he mastereth his mind, and directeth it to one point of concentration—holding at the same time his senses and wandering thoughts firmly in hand. Sitting thus steady and at rest, he doth purify his soul by directing his consciousness upon the Real Self—the Absolute which underlieth all.

"With his body well under control, according to the traditional customs of the Yogi, he gazeth undisturbed into the Eternal and Infinite, seeing naught of the world of sense around him. Serene, fearless and at peace —firm in his resolve—his mind, controlled and harmonized, is directed toward Me, to whom he aspireth. And, such a Yogi, thus united with his Real Self, and with mind thus controlled, passeth into that Peace and Bliss which is to be found in Me alone.

"Of a truth, to him who eateth like a glutton, or else maketh too much of a virtue of fasting, or who is too much inclined to sleep, or else who doth make a virtue of abstaining from sleep, cometh not the true Yogi knowledge. Such a one inclineth too much toward extremes, and departeth from the middle path of temperance. The Yogi knowledge, which destroyeth pain, cometh rather to him who observeth moderation and temperance in eating and recreation; in action and rest—who in fleeing from the evil of excess of action, doth not run into the twin evil of the excess of repression.

"When a man's thought, mastered by the Real Self, and fixed upon the Real Self, findeth itself free from lust and desire, then indeed hath that man gained the inward harmony which bringeth peace and satisfaction. Then doth his mind become stable and steady, like the flame of the lamp which resteth in the place where no wind cometh to disturb or cause it to flicker. Such a mind delighteth in the contemplation of the Real Self, and is well content to dwell in its peace and presence. Seeing the Real Self by the aid of its own light, it realizes that it has All, and is therefore satisfied.

"The Wise Man findeth his chief delight in that which is far above anything that the mind can obtain by means of the senses—and having found it, resteth in its Reality. Resting there in his new found realm, he knoweth well that beyond it there is no greater satisfaction; and being securely established in it, the greatest sorrows and griefs of the life of the world disturb not his peace or content, for he hath risen above them. This freedom from pain and sorrow, is known by the name of Yoga, which means Spiritual Union. Clasp it well to thee, O Prince, with firm resolution and with confident expectation.

"Casting behind thee the vain desires of the imagination; and mastering, by enlightened mind, the inclinations of the senses, step by step wilt thou attain tranquility and calm, by the exercise of the Awakened Mind, guided by the Spiritual. The mind once fixed upon the Real Self, it is folly for it to wander away from its Supreme Object. But if it doth, be thou vigilant to rein in the unruly steed, and by skillful guidance, lead it steadily back to where thou hast bidden it stand.

"The man, who hath attained this peace of mind, who hath gained this mastery of the carnal-mind, hath departed from that which

the world calls sin—hath escaped from error
—hath passed into the realm of Truth. Harmony of mind and soul—and the Blissful
State, is his. He seeth the Real Self in All—
and All in the Real Self. He seeth that One
is All, and All is One. Verily, say I unto
thee, that he who seeth Me in All, and All in
Me—him will I never forsake, nor will I suffer him to forsake me. Forever shall I bind
him to Me, with the golden fetters of Love,
which chafe not nor fret the soul. Yea even
say I that he who realizeth Me in my Unity,
and who loveth Me so, him shalt I cause to
live forever within my Being, even though he
appeareth to live separately in his own mode
of life, even in this world.

"The true Yogi, O Arjuna, is he who knoweth by what he hath found within himself,
that there is one underlying Essence pervading all life, and things; and recognizeth all
pain and pleasure as of equality and sameness
of nature. A great Yogi is such a one, O
Prince."

ARJUNA: "Alas, O *Krishna,* I am unable to
accept thy teaching of the steadfastness of
the controlled mind, of which thou hath

spoken. I know the mind to be most restless, unsteady, turbulent, strong and stubborn, obstinate, and not yielding readily to the Will. As well tell me to curb and control the wind, as it bloweth and passeth—now the gentle breeze, and now the raging storm—as to master and control with steady hand this mysterious principle which is called the Mind."

KRISHNA: "Well sayeth thou, O Prince, that the mind is restless and as difficult to restrain as the winds. Yet by constant practice, discipline and care may it be mastered. True it is that Yoga is most difficult of attainment, by a soul that is uncontrolled and that lacketh the touch of the hand of the master. But, nevertheless, the soul, when it has recognized the master-touch of the Real Self, may attain unto true Yoga by care and patience, coupled with firm resolution and determination."

ARJUNA: "What fate befalleth him, O Krishna, who though being filled with earnest faith, faileth to attain perfection in Yoga, because of his unmastered mind wandering away from the path of discipline and mastery? Doth he, thus standing between the merit of Right Action on one hand, and Spiritual Attainment on the other—lacking each support, and yet gaining not the other—doth he like a broken cloud, having severed its allegiance, and yet having failed to gain a new one, come to nothing and melt away to nothingness? Is he, standing thus confused in the very path of the Absolute, lost and forsaken? Answer me this my question, O Krishna, for it doth sore perplex me, and none other than Thee canst rightly inform me."

KRISHNA: "Know thou then, Arjuna, that such a one findeth not destruction either here nor in the worlds to come. His faith hath saved him alive—his goodness hath preserved him for annihiliation. The path of destruction is never for him who hath lived righteously, and with faith reached out toward Me. The man whose devotions and faith, attended by good works, were unattended by acquirement of the full discipline—such an one, I say, after death, cometh to a place of abode devoted to the righteous who have not as yet found deliverance. Dwelling there happily for an immensity of years, the soul is finally reborn in conditions and surroundings best adapted to the further attainment and unfoldment that await it.

"Perhaps, even, it may be reborn in the immediate family and company of some learned Yogi, although such a reward is bestowed only when fully deserved and called for by the Law. There, in the new life, doth he regain that which he hath acquired in the former life, and is thus enabled to take up the lesson where it was left off, and thereby advance gradually to a more perfect mastery.

"Nothing once gained is ever lost by death; the essence of attainment is preserved and re-bestowed upon the new born soul. His earnest reaching out for the attainment of Yoga, carrieth him even farther than would the mere study of the Sacred Writings. And, laboring with patience, perseverance and application, freed from his errors, and fully developed through many rebirths, he attaineth the goal he seeketh, and obtaineth Peace and Mastery.

"Thus thou seest that the faithful and earnest seeker after Truth—he who doth the best he can and ever trusts to the workings of the Law,—is greater by far than the fanatics who seek merit by penance and self-torture. Yea, also, better even, than many who call themselves learned, is he. And more merit hath he than many of those who seek merit by good works. Therefore, O *Arjuna,* become thou one who, with Faith and Love, letteth My love and life flow through him. Of all the Yogis, O Prince, I consider him the most devoted whose heart is filled to overflowing with love for Me, and who dwelleth in perfect Faith."

THUS ENDETH PART VI OF THE BHAGAVAD GITA. WHICH PART IS CALLED "SELF MASTERY."

PART VII.

SPIRITUAL DISCERNMENT.

Then, further unto *Arjuna,* spake *Krishna,* the Blessed Lord, saying:

"Listen now to My words, O *Arjuna,* and thou shalt learn how, having thy mind firmly fixed upon Me, and observing the Yogi teachings, thou shalt of a verity know Me without a doubt. I shall instruct thee in this wondrous wisdom and knowledge, without reserve or withholding, and when thou learnest this teaching, then shalt thou have acquired that knowledge which leaves nothing else to be known by man.

"But a few men, among the thousands of the race, have sufficient discernment to desire to attain Perfection. And of this few, the successful seekers are so rare, that there is but here one and there one who knoweth Me in my essential nature.

"In my nature are to be found the eightfold forms known as earth, water, fire, air, and ether, together with mind, reason and self-consciousness. But, besides these, I possess a higher and nobler nature—the nature or principle which supporteth and sustaineth the universe. Know this as the womb of creation.

"For I am the Creator of the universe—likewise am I the dissolution of the universe. Higher than I, there is naught. All the objects of the universe depend upon Me, and are sustained by Me, even as precious gems depend upon the thread which passeth through them holding all together and sustaining them.

"Moisture in the water am I, O Prince of Pandu—light of the sun and moon am I, O Prince—the Sacred Syllable, 'AUM' in the Vedas am I, O Companion in the Chariot—the sound-waves in the air; the virility in men; the perfume of the earth; the glowing flame in the fire, am I, O Warrior of the Pandus. Yea, even the very Life of all living things, am I, O Beloved—and likewise the very Yoga of the Yogis.

"Know thou, O Arjuna, that I am the eternal seed of all nature. I am the wisdom of the wise. I am the glory of the glorious. I am the strength of the strong. I am the love of Right Action, in those who follow the teachings of Service through Right Action. The three natures—the nature of harmony, the nature of activity, the nature of inactivity —these are in me, although I am not in them.

"The world of men, fallen under the illusion of these three qualities or natures, understandeth not that I am above these, standing untouched and unchanged, even amidst their countless changes and happenings. This illusion is most dense, and difficult of penetration by the eyes of men. But those there be who are able to see through the illusion, even unto the light of My flame which burns brightly beyond the enfolding garment of the smoke, and such come direct to Me.

"But there be many who cannot pierce the envelope of the smoke of illusion—such come not to Me; for they knoweth Me not; but they worship the gods of the material and sense-world, which alone seem Real to them.

"Among those who worship Me, O Prince, are four classes. I name them thus: the Distressed, the Seekers after Knowledge, the Seekers after Worldly Success, and the Wise Ones. Of these, the Wise Ones are the best; they recognize the One, and live in the world

of the One, doing its work with the light of
knowing. Such love Me much indeed; and
greatly loveth I them. Yea, holdeth these as
Myself, because they have blended themselves
with me, and find their lives in Me alone.

"After many lives, and with accumulated
wisdom, the Wise Ones come to Me, knowing
me to be All. Such are called *Mahatmas,*
and are rare and difficult to find by lesser
men. And the others, who are drawn away
through lack of understanding, to this deity,
or that one, with varying rites and ceremonies,
find other gods. They find that which they
seek, according to their natures.

"But, knoweth this, O Arjuna—and note it
well, for it is difficult of understanding among
those who are bigoted, fanatical and narrow
of mind and sympathy—the Truth is this:
that though men worship many gods, and
images, and hold many conceptions of Deity,
which they reverence as objects of worship—
yea, even though these men seem utterly opposed to each other, and to Me—yet doth their
faith arise from a latent and unfolded faith
in Me.

"Their faith in their gods and images is but

the dawning of faith in Me; in worshipping these forms and conceptions, they wish to worship Me, although they know it not. And, verily, say I unto you, such Faith and Worship, when honestly and conscientiously held and performed, shall not go unrewarded nor unaccepted by Me. Such men do the best possible to them, according to their light of dawning knowledge; and the benefits they seek, according to their faith, shall come to them, yea, even from Me. Such is my Love, Understanding and Justice.

"But, remembereth always this, O Prince, that these very rewards of finite desires, are likewise finite in the nature of things. The things these men pray for, are things of the moment—and things of the moment are given them as their reward. Those who worship the lesser gods—these distorted shadows of Me— pass into the shadow-worlds ruled over by these shadow-gods. But those who are wise, and are able to know Me as Myself—the All —the One—such come to Me in My world of Reality, where shadows are not, but where all is Real, even as the Flame which casteth the shadow.

"There be those, who lacking in Discernment, think of Me as being Manifest and visible to their eyes. Know thou, Arjuna, that in my essence I am not manifest or visible to men. Back of my emanated forms, rest I, undiscovered and invisible to the ignorant. Birthless and deathless am I—though the smoke-blinded world discerneth this not, for they take the shadow for the substance. Full well knoweth I the countless beings which have passed before my gaze, on the broad field of the universe, in the misty path. Likewise, knoweth I all who are now present on the field. And, moreover—mighty mystery this to men, O Prince—I also know all that shall hereafter tread the field. But of them all—past, present and future—not one fully knoweth Me. I hold them all in my mind, but their minds cannot hold Me in my essence.

"Blinded by the pairs of opposites, O Prince their eyes filled with the smoke of illusion—seeking instead of Unity, the opposing forms of like and dislike; men walk in the field of the Universe, deluded, all. Nay, not all—for there be a few who have freed themselves from the pair of opposites—who have discarded attachment—who have cleared their eyes of the smoke of illusion; such as these, O Prince, know Me to be the One—the All—and hold to Me, steadfast and constant, in their love and devotion.

"They who have thus found Me cling to Me, even as a babe clingeth to the breast of the mother. They move ever onward toward deliverance and attainment—they know the Real Self—the Eternal—the Infinite—the Absolute—the One—Myself! They know My works. They know My Wisdom. They know My Lordship of All in All. They know that all Life is Mine—that all worship comes to Me. With steadfast minds, and hearts overflowing with love for Me, they know Me in life—yea, even in the hour of the passing of their souls from their wornout bodies, such know Me."

THUS ENDETH PART VII OF THE BHAGAVAD GITA, WHICH PART IS CALLED "SPIRITUAL DISCERNMENT."

PART VIII.

Yet again, spake *Arjuna,* unto *Krishna,* the Blessed Lord, saying:

"Tell me, I pray Thee, O *Krishna,* My Beloved Teacher, what is the Universal Life? And what is that which we call Self-consciousness? And what is the essential nature of Action? And what is the constitution of the Universal Principles? And what is that knowledge of the Arch-angelic hosts, higher far than that of man? And what is the secret of Thine appearance in the body? Inform me of all these things, O Wisest of Teachers, and further tell me how the Wise Ones know Thee at the hour of death?"

KRISHNA: "I am the All, from which All proceedeth. From Me floweth out the Soul of Souls—the Universal Life—the One Life of the Universe. *Karma,* which many call the essence of Action, is that principle of my emanation which causeth things to live, and move and act. The Universal Principles, in

their inner constitution, are but my Will
manifested in the Natural laws of the universe. The knowledge of the Arch-angelic
hosts is the knowledge of the Spirit. The
secret of Mine appearance in the flesh, belongeth to those who are able to understand the
higher teachings, and is closely woven with
the Law of Sacrifice.

"At the hour of death, the Wise One, with
mind fixed upon me, goeth straight to Me,
without doubt or mischance. But, he who fas-
teneth his desire upon aught else—if there be
to him a greater god, material or otherwise,
than Me—to that god of materiality, or super-
materiality, goeth that man. Each goeth to
that which is his Ruling Passion, strong even
in the hour of death. Therefore, make Me
thy Ruling Passion, even unto the hour of
death, and then fight the fight that is before
thee.

"With thy mind and understanding fixed
firmly upon Me, of a certainty shalt thou
come to Me. To the Spirit goeth he, who, setting aside all other desire, liveth the life of
the Spirit by constant Right Thinking and

Right Action; to the Spirit goeth he who is of the Spirit.

"He who thinketh, with enlightened mind, of the Eternal as the All Wise, the All Powerful, the infinitely small, the infinitely large—the underlying sustainer of all—the invisible essence,—the opposer of darkness—with a mind fixed steadily upon the task, and with his vital powers devoted to the one end—passeth to the Spirit Divine and Imperishable.

"There is a Path to Spirit, which those well-learned in the *Vedas,* (or Sacred Writings,) call the Imperishable.—that Path upon which the strong men, who have mastered their minds and controlled their passions, seek to tread—that Path which is chosen by those who take the vow of continence, and asceticism, and godly study and thought. Listen, and I will inform thee of this Path.

"Close tightly those gates of the body, which men call the avenues of the senses. Concentrate thy mind upon thine inner self. Let thine 'I' dwell, in full strength, within its abode, not seeking to move outward. Stand firm, fortified by thy Yogi power, and repeat in The Silence, the mystic syllable 'Aum' (the symbol of My Being as Creator, Preserver, and Destroyer, according to the letters or sounds thereof). Then, faithful to this, when thou quittest thy mortal frame, with thy thoughts fixed upon Me, shalt thou pass on to the Path of Supreme Bliss.

"He who thinketh constantly and fixedly of Me, O Prince, letting not his mind ever stray toward another object, will be able to find Me without overmuch trouble—yea, he will find me, will that devoted one.

"Once having reaohed Me, those Wise Ones need come not again to earthly birth—that plane of pain and finitude. Nay, indeed, there be no need of this for them, for they have passed beyond these lower planes and reached the plane of Bliss.

"The worlds and universes—yea, even the world of *Brahm,* a single day of which is like unto a thousand *Yugas,* (four billion years of the earth,) and his night as much—these worlds must come and go, but, even when they pass, and pass again, the souls of the Wise Ones who reach Me, return not.

"The days of *Brahm,* are succeeded by the nights of *Brahm.* In *Brahmic* days all things emerge from invisibility and become visible. And on the coming of the *Brahmic* Night, all visible things again melt into invisibility. The universe, having once existed, melteth away; but lo! is again re-created. But there existeth that which is higher than visibility or invisibility, and such is called the Unmanifest and Imperishable.

"On this Highest Path, then, O Prince, is found the way to that which is Unmanifest and Indestructible, and which when once reached is forever gained, without danger of loss. It is My Supreme Abode.

"The Spirit may be reached by those of the Spirit alone—those who have no other longing—those who have no other gods to worship. In this Spirit is enfolded all Nature and universes. From It proceedeth all things, flowing out in accordance to My Will.

"I would tell thee, O Prince, of that time of death, in which men, passing out, shall never return; and of that time of death, in which they, passing out, shalt again return to earth. He who departeth in the Light returneth not to this plane of pain. But he who departeth in the Darkness, returneth he to mortal re-birth,

again and again, until he findeth the Light.
The true *Yogi* understandeth this saying, O
Prince!

"Therefore, perfecteth thyself in *Yoga*, O
Arjuna, Prince of Pandu! The fruit of this
knowledge, *Arjuna*, surpasseth all the rewards
of virtue, as pointed out to the students of the
Sacred Writings; of all worshippings; all sacrifices; all austerities; all alms-giving, even
great though these be. The *Yogi*, learned in
the knowledge of the Truth, passeth beyond
these, and taketh precedence to those who follow them; he reacheth the Supreme Goal.

THUS ENDETH PART VIII, OF THE BHAGAVAD
GITA, WHICH PART IS CALLED THE "MYSTERY
OF OMNIPRESENCE."

PART IX.

THE KINGLY KNOWLEDGE.

Then spake *Krishna,* the Blessed Lord, unto Prince *Arjuna,* saying:

"And, now giveth I to thee, O *Arjuna,* thou faithful and trusting one, the final and supreme knowledge—the wisdom royal—whose secret, when once known to thee, O Prince, shalt set thee free from evil and misfortune. This is the true Kingly Science—Royal Secret —Imperial Purifier—most easy of intuitional comprehension to such as thou art—not difficult of performance—and imperishable and never-failing. Those who possess not this knowledge fail to find Me, and therefore return again and again to this world of birth and death.

"This universe, in its parts, and in its entirety, is an emanation of Me, and I fill it in my invisible form—yea, even I, the Unmanifest. All things are of Me—not I of them. But, mistake thou not, O Prince, lest thou in error think that even All Things *are* Myself.

I am the sustainer of all things, but All Things are not I. Knoweth thou that even as the vast volume of Air, everywhere present, and in constant activity, is sustained and contained within the Universal Ether—so do all manifested things rest in Me, the Unmanifest. This is the Secret, O Arjuna; ponder well upon it. At the end of a *Kalpa*—a day of *Brahm*—a period of creative activity—I withdraw into my nature all things and beings. And, at the beginning of another *Kalpa, I* emanate all things and beings, and re-perform my creative act. Throughout Nature, which too is mine own, I emanate, again and again, all these things that constitute the universe, by the power of this Nature, which by itself is without power.

"But I am not bound or entangled in these works, O Prince, for I sit on high, unattached and unbound by actions. I super-impose my power upon nature, and she builds up and tears down—producing the animate and the inaminate; and thus the universal action proceeds and operates.

"The unenlightened, seeing Me in human form, and being ignorant of My true nature

as Supreme Lord of All, disregard me, and
hold me in but small esteem. Such hold to
vain hopes and petty actions; they lack wisdom, and live on the lower planes of their
being, the evil, brutal and deceitful nature
being their highest development.

"But the Wise Ones, they who have unfolded their higher natures, know Me to be
the Infinite and Eternal Origin of All Things,
and they worship Me with single-mind.
Always realizing My Power, such worship Me
continually, firm in their faith, and earnest in
their devotion, being not diverted or tempted
toward other worship or devotion. Others see
Me in various forms and aspects, and thus
worship Me in various ways. Both as the
One and as the Many am I worshipped.

"Yea, in all worship am I. Yea, verily, indeed, I *am* the worship; I am the sacrifice; I
am the libation offered the souls of the ancestors; I am the sacrificial spices; I am the
prayers and invocation; I am the *mantram;* I
am the burnt offering and the butter sacrificed
to the gods; I am the fire that consumes the
offering; I am that which is consumed by
the fire. Yea, also am I the Father of the

universe—and likewise the Mother. I am the
Preserver. I am the Holy One whom all seek
to know. I am the mystic word *'Aum.'* I am
the three sacred books or *Vedas*—the *Rik,
Samur* and *Yajur*.

"Even so, am I the Path; the Comforter;
the Creator; the Witness; the Resting Place;
the Place of Refuge; and the Friend of All.
I am the Origin and the End—the Creation
and the Destruction—the Store-house—the
Eternal Seed. I am the Sunshine—I am the
Rain. I now press out, and I now draw in.
I am Death, and yet am I Immortality. I am
Being and yet am I Non-Being. I am the
One beyond both.

"Those learned in the three *Vedas,* offering
many sacrifices, drinking the sacred *Soma*
juice at the end of the sacrifice, and thus seeking purification, according to the ancient rites
—in reality pray to Me beseeching me to point
out the Way to Heaven. And thus gain they
their desired Heavenly Realm, and partake
of the celestial foods, and enter into the
divine enjoyments.

"But, when they have partaken of the heavenly feasts, and the divine enjoyments, and

have entered into the pleasures of that vast Heaven-world, and have thus exhausted the reward for their good deeds, virtues, and worship—then are they carried back by the Law, to re-birth in this plane of sorrow which we call the earth. They have followed the finite and transitory road, and have received the finite and transitory reward. Following the precepts of the *Vedas,* and becoming good worshippers and observers of forms, they come to desire these rewards—and their desires blossom into the fruit of realization, each according to its kind. Transitory and finite desires blossom into finite rewards

"But, he who holdeth Me constantly in mind and serveth no other will be brought through safely; for him *I* perform the sacrifice and ceremonies. He is mine own!

"But, again, remember, O Prince, that even those who worship other gods, worship Me, though they realize it not. If they be full of love and faith, I accept it as intended for Me, and give to such their reward according to their merit and desires. But although all such worship Me, and are rewarded accordingly, yet because of their lack of knowledge of Me in my Essence, they must in due time relinquish Heaven, and return again to earth in re-birth.

"Each goeth to that which he worshipeth, according to his degree of spiritual comprehension. Those who worship personal gods, or angels, go to dwell with personal gods and angels; those who worship ancestors, go to dwell with the ancestors; those who worship spirits, go to the land of spirits. And those who worship Me, in my Essence, come to dwell with Me in my Essence.

"But know thou, *Arjuna,* that I despise not the worship of the humble and simple folk, who in their loving worship present Me with leaves, flowers, fruits and water. I say unto thee that I accept and enjoy such offerings from these, my children; in the spirit of the gift do I accept it. All sacrifices I accepteth, even in the spirit of the offering, not in the value of the gift. Therefore, whatever thou dost, O Prince, whether it be eating, giving, sacrificing, or performance of ceremonies or rites—do these things in earnest offering to Me. And offering up to Me all thy works, thou shalt be delivered, and set free from the

bonds of action and the consequences thereof.
Thy mind thus having become evenly balanced
and harmonized, to me shalt thou come at the
appointed time.

"I see My children of the world—all living
beings—with an equal eye, and without par-
tiality. There is none more dear to me than
another, nor less dear. None do I love more,
or hate more, than any other one. Those who
worship me with devotion, verily they findeth
for themselves the road to my heart, and I am
in them, and they in Me. If one who is most
evil turneth to Me with undivided heart, he
hath started toward Me on the Path of Righteousness. And, if he persisteth in his righteous resolve, O *Arjuna,* he cannot escape becoming virtuous, and he shall obtain the
Peace, even as shall the pious man.

"Know for a certainty, O *Arjuna,* that he
who is my faithful servant perishes not. All
who seek sanctuary in Me, O Prince of Pandu—even those born of the womb of sin; and
those whom the priests tell us are beyond the
pale—yea, even such shall tread the highest
paths, if they but place their hopes and faith
upon Me. And if this be so, O Prince, how

certain is the salvation of the holy men, and learned souls.

"Then, regard this earth as but a finite and transitory abode, and know and worship Me, Fix upon Me, without distraction thine earnest mind, and thou shalt come unto me—yea, shalt thou be blended into Me and thus reach the Supreme Goal."

THUS ENDETH PART IX OF THE BHAGAVAD GITA, WHICH PART IS CALLED "THE KINGLY KNOWLEDGE."

PART X.

UNIVERSAL PERFECTION.

Then, *Krishna,* the Blessed Lord, unto *Arjuna,* Prince of the Pandus, in these words, spoke further:

"Hearken to my words, Thou Strong-armed One of Pandu, while I inform thee of My supreme teachings, desiring thy welfare. For know thou that thou art beloved of Me, O *Arjuna.*

"Knoweth thou that neither the angels, nor gods, nor great spirits, nor adepts, nor others high in knowledge, know aught of my Beginning; for even before angels and gods and great spirits or adepts was I, yea, even am I *their* Beginning. He, who, in his wisdom, knoweth Me to be birthless and beginningless —eternal—without commencement—the Supreme Lord of all that came afterward from Me—he, being free from illusion and error, shall be free from the consequences of sin.

"Know thou those things that are named: Reason, Knowledge, Wisdom,

Patience; Truth; Forgiveness; Self-mastery; Calmness; Pleasure and Pain; Birth and Death; Courage and Fear; Mercy; Joy; Charity; Earnestness; Fame and Infamy; all these various qualities of Personalities flow forth from Me. Even so came the seven great Sages; and the four original Beings, or Manus; all emanated from my Mind—and from these sprang the race which people the world. He who knoweth this truth regarding My sovereignty and essential super-universality, is, without doubt, endowed with the spring or unerring and intelligent faith and devotion.

"I am the Emanator of all this—all things flow from me. Knowing this as the Truth, the Wise Ones revere and worship Me with rapt souls. With Me ever in mind, and with Me ever occupying the sacred chamber of their hearts, they are filled with a secret joy and calm content. And from within the minds and hearts of such, I constantly illuminate and inspire them, so that they are a constant source of inspiration to each other, and their inward lights combine to shine forth to the world of darkness and ignorance. To such as these, of even mind and faith, I give Discrimination and Spiritual Insight, and they unfold unto Spiritual Consciousness, by which they know and come unto Me.

"From My great love for these, my faithful ones, I shine forth from within them, in the light of the Spirit, and the dark places of ignorance, which existed in their minds, are thus made light and shining with Wisdom."

ARJUNA: "Verily art thou the Supreme Lord—*Parabrahm*—beyond even great Brahm art Thou. The gods, sages, angels, and wise souls, acknowledge Thee to be the Supreme Abode, the Supreme Eternal One, the Infinite Pure One, the Absolute Being, Omnipotent, Omnipresent, Omniscient—and now hath Thou likewise proclaimed the Truth of these sayings to me. And verily do I believe Thee, in full and without reserve, O Blessed Lord of All. Thy present incarnate manifestation —that mighty mystery of thy presence in earthly form—is understood not, even by the gods, and angels, and mighty souls of all the worlds. Only thyself, understandest Thyself. Thou Fount of Life; Thou Supreme Lord of All the Universe of Universes; God of gods;

Master and Ruler of All that is, has been, or ever will be—without Beginning and without End—without Limits on any side—this and infinitely more art Thou, O Blessed One!

"I, thine unworthy pupil, pray thee to condescend to inform me by what wondrous power hast Thou pervaded all the universe, and yet remained Thyself? How shalt I, although constantly worshipping Thee, ever come to know Thee? How shalt I think of Thee—how shalt Thou be meditated upon O Lord, when I knoweth not Thy proper form? Tell me, fully, I pray Thee, of Thy powers and forms of manifestation—of Thy distinctions and glorious condescensions. For, verily, do I thirst for such knowledge, even as one thirsteth for the living waters—for Thy words are to me like the clear waters which quench the thirst of him to whom water hath been denied for many days. Give me the blessing of thy words, O Lord!"

KRISHNA: "My Blessings and Peace to thee, O Beloved Prince! I will acquaint thee with the chief of my divine distinctions, and manifestations—this must suffice, for know thou that my essential nature and being is infinite.

"I, O Prince, am the Spirit which is well-seated in the consciousness of all beings, the reflection of which they each know as 'I,' or the Ego. I am the Beginning, the Middle, and also the Ending, of all things. Among the Sun-gods, I am the Supreme Creator. Among the shining suns, I am the Supreme Sun. I am the Supreme Mover of the Winds. Among the stars, I am the Moon which out-shines them. Among the *Vedas,* or sacred books, I am the Highest Book, or Book of Song. I am the Super-god. I am the Mind. I am the Life.

"Among the attributes of fate, I am Fate. Among the genii of good fortune and bad fortune, I am Fortune. Among the Original I am the Original Being. Among the teach-ers, I am the Teacher of the Divine Teach-ers. Among the generals, I am the Leader of the Celestial Armies. Among the bodies of waters, I am the Ocean. Among the Wise Ones, I am Wisdom. Among the words, I am the sacred syllable Aum. Among wor-shipers, I am the Name of God. Among the hills, I am the *Himalayas*. I am the Sage of Sages. I am the Saint.

"Among the horses, I am the Mighty Horse who arose with the *Amrita* from the ocean. Among men, I am the Emperor of Emperors. Among weapons, I am the Divine Thunderbolt. Among lovers, I am Love. Among serpents, I am the Eternal Serpent, the joined ends of which are a symbol of the beginningless and endless ring of eternity. Among the creatures of the deep, I am the God of the Ocean. I am the Judge of the Day of Judgment. I am Spirit.

"I am Eternity. Among the beasts, I am the Lion. Among the birds, I am *Vainateya,* the bird of the fabulous stories, whose wings extend even unto the ends of the earth. Among purifiers, I am the Pure Air. Among those who carry arms, I am the Lord of Arms. Among the fishes, I am *Makara,* the mighty fish of the legends. Among rivers, I am the Sacred *Ganges*. Of changeful things, I am the Beginning, the Middle, and the End. I am Absolute Knowledge.

"And, also, am I the never-failing Preserver, whose gaze is turned in all directions, and

who allows none to perish. And, also am I
Death, from whose visits none are exempt.
And, likewise, am I the Re-birth, which dis-
solves Death. I am Fame; Fortune; Elo-
quence; Memory; Understanding; Fortitude;
and Patience. Among hymns, I am the
Hymn of Hymns, or *Brihat Sama.* And
among harmonious metres, I am the *Gaya-
tree,* or most harmonious. Among the sea-
sons, I am the Season of Flowers. The
Splendor of splendid things, am I. And Victory am I; and Earnestness; and Determination; and the Truth of the truthful.

"I am the Head of the great clans and
families. I am the Sage of the sages; the
Poet of the poets; the Bard of bards; Seer of
seers; Prophet of prophets. To rulers of
men, I am the Sceptre of Power. Among
statesmen and those who seek to conquer, I
am Statescraft and Policy. Among the secre-
tive I am Silence. I am Wisdom.

"In short, and most briefly stated, O Prince,
I am THAT which is the essential principle in
the seed of all beings and things in nature;
and everything whether animate or inanimate
is infilled with me—without Me nothing could

exist for even the twinkling of an eye, O Prince.

"There is no end to my manifestations, O Arjuna—my powers are infinite in quality and variety. Every being or thing that can be known is the product of an infinitesimal portion of my power and glory. Those which I have mentioned are but trifling examples of the same. Whatever is known to thee as existing, know that as being a tiny manifestation of my infinite power and glory.

"But why concern thyself with all this knowledge, and all these instances? *Know thou, Arjuna, that I manifested all this Universe with but an infinitesimal fragment of Myself—and still I remain, its Lord, unattached and apart, although pervading all.*"

THUS ENDETH PART X OF THE BHAGAVAD GITA, WHICH PART IS CALLED "UNIVERSAL PERFECTION."

PART XI.

THE UNIVERSAL MANIFESTATION.

Then spake *Arjuna,* unto the Blessed Lord, *Krishna,* saying:

"Thou hast removed my illusion and ignorance, by thy words of Wisdom, regarding the Supreme Mystery of the Spirit, which thou hast spoken unto me out of Thy great love and compassion. From thee have I learned the full truth regarding the creation and destruction of all things; and also concerning Thy greatness and all-embracing immanence. Thou art indeed the Lord of All, even as thou describeth Thyself. But, one final token of Thy love for me, I beg of Thee, O Lord and Master. I would, if such be possible for me, that Thou showeth unto me Thine own Countenance and Form—the Imperishable Spirit."

KRISHNA: "Since thou asketh me for this, O *Arjuna,* even shalt it be granted thee. Behold then, O Prince, my millions of forms divine, of all shapes and forms, species, colors and kinds. Behold thou first the numberless heavenly hosts and celestial beings—angels; arch-angels; planetary gods; rulers of universes; and many other wonderful and mighty beings scarce dreamt of in thy wildest speculations and fancies, O Arjuna.

"Then behold as a Unity, standing within My body, the whole Universe, animate and inanimate, and all things else that thy mind impelleth thee to see. Exercise thy fullest desires and hopes, and even thine imagination, and lo! all that thou hast desired, or hoped for, or even imagineth, that shalt thou see within Me. But not with thine natural human eye see these things, O Arjuna, for they are finite and imperfect. But now I endow thee with the Eye of the Spirit with which thou mayest see the glorious sight awaiting thee."

Then, having thus spoken, *Krishna,* the Blessed Lord of Lords, showed himself to *Arjuna* in the aspect of the Supreme and Absolute, through Its manifestations. And this aspect showed itself as Many within the One. The Many had millions of eyes and mouths; many wonderful appearances; many forms of upraised weapons; many forms of clothing and array, jewels and vestments. The Face of faces was turned everywhere, and in all directions. The glory and radiance of a million suns would pale into insignificance before that vision of the Mighty Face.

Then saw *Arjuna* the Universe separated into its manifold parts and varieties, as One within the body of *Krishna,* the Lord of All. And the Prince of the Pandus, was overcome with awe and wonder, and each hair upon his head extended itself erect, like unto the blades of grass in the field. Then with hands joined together, in the attitude of reverence and devotion, he bowed his head before the Lord, saying:

"O Mighty Lord, within Thy form I seeth the lesser gods and arch-angels, and angels, and all the heavenly hosts of greater and lesser degree. Within Thee I see even *Brahma,* the Creator, sitting on his lotus throne, surrounded by the revered Sages and the Wise Ones. And, on all sides, in infinite variety, I see the countless forms of all living beings. With millions of arms, eyes, and bodies, ap-

peareth Thou to me, but even so I fail to discover Thy beginning, middle or end.

"I see Thee with crown of Universal Glory,
armed with the Universal weapons of mighty
power. And darting from Thee, on all sides,
I see wondrous beams of effulgent radiance
and glorious brilliancy. Difficult indeed is it
to see Thee at all, for the light, like unto the
rays of a million-million suns, multiplied and
magnified a million-million times, dazzleth
even the divine eye with which thou hast
endowed me. Verily, indeed, art Thou the
Supreme Lord—ever immanent—containing
all that is; or can be thought of or known.
Thou art indeed the Preserver and Supporter
of the Universe. Thou art indeed the Fount
of Wisdom! Thou art indeed the Ancient of
Days, and the Beginningless One! Spirit of
Spirit, art Thou! Yea, Thou art The AB-
SOLUTE!

"Without beginning, middle, or ending—
with infinite arms—with infinite power—with
eyes like unto the sun—with radiance flowing
from Thee and filling the entire universe—
thus I behold Thee. The heavens and the
earth, and all the space that is between and

around them is filled by Thee alone, and every point and corner containeth Thee! The Three Worlds behold thy Awful Countenance with awe and bewilderment.

"Flying to Thee for refuge and haven, seeth I pouring in the wondrous bands of the heavenly hosts, with joined palms and reverent attitude. Cometh all the heavenly hosts of celestial beings, whom men call by the many names of *Mararshis; Siddhas; Rudras; Adityas; Vasus; Vishvas; Ashvins; Kumars; Maruts; Ushmapas; Gandharvas; Yakshas; Asuras,* and all the other hosts of the celestial and heavenly worlds, regions and planes; all pouring into Thee as the rivers into the ocean —all gazing upon Thy Being with wonder and amazement!

"I seeth the many worlds standing awe-struck and amazed at the sight of Thy wondrous manifestations.

"I see Thee touching the very heavens, and shining forth with glorious radiance, of all hues, shades and colors. My resolution faileth me, and I am without calm and peace. I see Thy awful countenance appearing as dreadful as Eternity. And then would I fly from Thee, but nowhere can I go where I can escape the sight of Thy awful presence—nowhere is there a Place outside of the All. Have mercy upon me then, O Lord and All, Thou harborer of the Universe!

"Ah, now, seeth I the sons of *Dhritarashtra,* the Kuru Princes, and with them the thousand others of earthly kings and rulers. With them come *Bhishma* and *Drona,* and the mighty warriors of the hosts. O, horror of horrors! even as I gazeth upon them, I see the battlehosts rushing into Thy gaping, fiery mouths and frightful rows of teeth! Yea, many are caught between Thy teeth, and are mangled and ground to a pulp.

"Even as the floods from swollen streams pour tumultuously into the sea, so pour and rush these living streams of warriors into Thy flaming mouths, with much haste, as if seeking their own destruction. Yea, even as the evening moths, in great number, fly with quickening speed, and find their destruction in the bright flame, so do these generals, chiefs and warriors pour into Thy flaming mouths, and are consumed and reduced unto dust and powder.

"I see Thee, with thy blazing mouths, drawing in, devouring, swallowing and consuming all mankind, on all sides, and without limit, while thy fiery beams shine forth with dreadful force filling the Universe. Verily, Thou consumeth the worlds, O *Krishna,* Lord of All! Prostrate before Thee I fall, and with joined palms I pray to Thee, O Lord! But even as I pray in awe of Thee—yet do I beg of Thee to inform me what is this that I see in Thee? Where and what are Thou, in thine Own Aspect?"

KRISHNA: "Thou seest me as Time, fully matured and complete—the Destroyer of Mankind—who cometh hither to seize and consume all those who stand before Me. Knoweth thou, that excepting thyself who shall be saved, not one of these many warriors ranged here in battle array, confronting each other with fierce resolve—yea, not even one else shall escape Me.

"Wherefore arise and fight thy fight! Play well thy part as warrior and chief! Win for thyself the renown and fame of battle! Conquer thy foes! Enter into and enjoy the conquered kingdom! For know that, by me,

already art they overcome and conquered—
thou art only mine immediate agent—the instrument to execute the decree of that which
men call Fate. Then do thou slay *Drona,* and
Bhishma, and *Jayadratha,* and *Karna,* and all
the other warriors of the field, for they are already killed by Me in Destiny and Law. Fight
then without fear or holding back, and thou
shalt destroy thy rivals and enemies of the
opposing hosts! Fight, *Arjuna*—Fight!"

Then *Arjuna,* the Pandu Prince, having
heard these words of *Krishna,* the Blessed
Lord, fell prostrate before the Lord, with
joined palms, and with devout demeanor.
And addressing the Lord, in broken acents
spake he thus:

"O *Krishna, Krishna*—Blessed Lord—the
universe rejoiceth and is filled with thy power
and glory! The evil spirits flee in terror from
thy sight—and the hosts of the Holy Ones
sing thy praises, and adore Thee with awe and
wonder! And wherefore, O Lord, should not
all mighty beings bow before thee in adoration
and awe-struck humility, for art Thou not the
Being of Beings—the Mighty of the Mighty—
the *Brahm* of *Brahma*—the Supreme Creator

—the Eternal God of Gods—the World containing the worlds? Being and No-Being art Thou, and even That which lieth back of both. Thou art the Infinite, Eternal Absolute! Thou art the Supporter of All! Thou art the Spirit of the Spirit! Thou art All Wisdom known, and all Wisdom possessing—Wisdom Absolute art Thou! Thou art the dwelling-place of universes—and by Thee was the universe emanated and spread out! *Vaya,* the god of wind —*Agni* the god of fire—*Varuna* the god of oceans—*Sashanka* the moon—*Prajapati* the god of nations—*Prapitamaha* the common ancestor of the race—all these art Thou, O *Krishna,* my Lord and Love—Reverence a thousand times multiplied and magnified be unto Thee. Reverence to Thee a million-million times repeated. Again and again a million-million times, be this repeated reverence be Thine, O Infinite One! On all sides of Thee, reverence and worship! Before and behind Thee, reverence! O Omnipotent, Omnipresent, Omniscient One, who art All in All! Infinite is thy Glory! Thou includeth within Thyself All Things—wherefore art Thou All Things, and more than All Things!

"Alas, alas! in my ignorance, O Lord, and regarding thee merely as my friend, I have called Thee with familiarity, saying: 'O *Krishna;* O Friend!' and other names of familiar intercourse. Thus did I address Thee, in my ignorant love and esteem and brotherly feeling. Unknowing of Thy real nature and greatness was I, hence my error—hence my great presumption. And, Thou, even Thou hath been treated by me with irreverence and undue familiarity, even at play and at sports; in public upon many and various occasions— for all of which, O Being Absolute and Infinite, I humbly beg thy forgiveness and pardon.

"Thou art the Parent of the animate and inanimate! Thou art the Wise Instructor of all who seek wisdom! Thou art the One alone worthy to be adored! Thou art the One like whom there is none! Yea, in all the three worlds there is none like unto Thee! Wherefore, bow down to the very earth, myself do I, and crave thy forgiving mercy and compassion. Lord, Lord, *Krishna,* My Lord!

Adorable Lord! bear with me even as a
father beareth with his son; a friend with a
friend; a lover with his beloved—so bear with
me, O Lord!

"Most favored am I in being shown that
which no man hath ever yet seen—and most
happy am I to have been so favored, and to
have witnessed these things, O Lord; yea, even
when I remembereth that which I have seen,
my heart beateth strongly, and my breath cometh and goeth rapidly, so overwhelmed doth
my mind become. And, yet, even from my
awe doth my words spring, when I beg of
Thee still another gift; I beseech Thee to
show me Thyself in Thy Celestial Form. Assume then, O Thousand armed One—Universal Former of Form—assume Thou then, I
pray Thee, Thy familiar shape in which I
have seen Thee countless times, and upon
which I can look without so great fear."

KRISHNA: *"Arjuna,* out of my love and
affection for thee, hath I shown thee, by my
divine power, this my supreme forms as the
Universe, in all its splendid glory, eternal and
infinite. None other than thyself hath ever
seen this sight. For know you this, that no

such sight can be obtained as a reward, even by the study of the *Vedas;* or by sacrifice; or by great learning; or by charity and alms-giving; or by good deeds; or by penance and self-denial. Not even these things, great as they may be and are, can win for a reward this vision and sight of Me which hath been granted unto thee, alone in all the three worlds. Having, witnessing these things—beheld My form, so awful to thee—be not dismayed, nor confounded or confused in thy faculties. When thy mind hath been quieted in its fears, and peace and calmness again cometh to thee, then mayest thou again behold My wondrous form!"

Then *Krishna,* the blessed Lord, having thus reassured *Arjuna,* resumed his milder and less terrible shape and consoled *Arjuna's* terrified mind. And, thus reassured and comforted, and his fears having departed, *Arjuna* spake to *Krishna,* saying:

"Beholding again thy less terrible shape, O Lord, I am again myself and in calmer frame of mind and less disturbed."

KRISHNA: "Yea, O *Arjuna,* hast thou beheld my wondrous form, which even the gods and arch-angels and the higher heavenly host ever long with earnest craving to witness and behold. But such can see me not, as thou hast seen me. Nay not even through the *Vedas,* nor by self-denial, nor by gifts of charity, nor by sacrifices. But by supreme devotion to Me alone, may I thus be perceived, O Prince, and he who thus perceiveth men and knoweth Me, verily he entereth into my essence and is enfolded by Me. He who doeth actions for Me alone—whose Supreme Good I am—My true devotee, freed from attachment to all but Me —regardless of consequences—free from hatred of any being or thing whatsoever— verily I say he cometh unto Me, O *Arjuna;* he cometh unto Me."

THUS ENDETH PART XI OF THE BHAGAVAD GITA, WHICH PART IS CALLED "THE UNIVERSAL MANIFESTATION."

PART XII.

Once again, *Krishna,* the Blessed Lord, spake to *Arjuna,* saying:

"Tell me, O Lord, which of those who worship and serve thee, with earnest minds well-mastered, as Thou hath just mentioned to me—which of such serve Thee most worthily and best? Which are on the best path, those who worship Thee as God in thy revealed form, on the one hand; or those who worship Thee as The Absolute—The Unmanifest—The Infinite—on the other hand? Which of these two classes of *Yogis* are more deeply versed in *Yoga?*"

KRISHNA: "Those, who have concentrated their minds fixedly upon me as God, and who serve Me with unwavering zeal and impregnable and steady faith—are regarded by Me as being most devoted. But, also, those who worship Me as The Absolute; The Infinite; The Unmanifest; The Omnipresent, Omnipotent, Omniscient; The Unknowable; The Un-

123

thinkable; The Ineffable; The Invisible; The
Eternal; The Immutable; The All; or as THAT
to which similar terms attempting to express
similar conceptions of Being are applied—such
so worshipping, and mastering the mind and
senses, and regarding all things in nature as
good and deserving to fare well, and rejoicing
in the welfare of all, equally—verily, these
also cometh unto Me.

"The path of those who are attracted by Me
as the Absolute and Unmanifest is much
harder to travel than is that of those who worship Me as God manifest, and having form.
This Absolute conception is most difficult of
realization to the finite mind of man. It is
most difficult for the visible to realize the invisible—the finite, the infinite—the possessor
of qualities and attributes, THAT which hath
neither but yet is above both.

"And, this also, say I to thee, O *Arjuna,* that
those also who, fixing their minds solely
upon me, and seeing in Me the Actor of actions, worship Me single-mindedly without
fear or hope of reward, them too shall I raise
up from the ocean of change and mortality.

"Place thy mind firmly upon Me, O Prince,

and let thine understanding penetrate into My being, and then, of a truth, shalt thou enter into Me, hereafter. But if thou art not able to hold thy mind firmly fixed upon Me, *Arjuna*, then seek to reach Me by the path of Practice and Discipline. And if even by Practice and Discipline thou art still unable to attain, then shalt thou seek me by the path of Service through Right Action. For by the performance of Right Actions, solely for My sake, shalt thou then attain perfection.

"And, if even this last task shall be beyond thy powers, then shalt thou follow the path of Renunciation, and putting thy trust earnestly upon Me, renounce thou the fruit of every action.

"Better, truly, is Wisdom and Knowledge than Practice and Discipline; and Meditation is still better than even Knowledge; and Renunciation is better than Meditation, for Renunciation of the fruits of action bringeth peace and satisfaction.

"Verily, I say unto Thee, that he is very dear and near to Me, who harboreth no malice or ill-will to any being or thing; who is the friend and lover of all Nature, who is merciful, free from pride and vanity and selfishness; who is undisturbed by pleasure or pain, being balanced in each; who is patient under wrongs and injustice and who is forgiving, contented, ever devout, with mind, senses and passions ever under control, and whose mind and understanding is ever fixed upon Me.

"He, also, is dear to Me, who neither fears the world of men, nor is feared by it; and who is delivered from the turbulence of anger, joy, impatience, or fear, regarding finite things or happenings.

"And he who desireth nothing; who is just and pure; impartial; free from anxieties; and who hath abandoned all finite rewards or hopes of rewards, is also dear to me. Likewise he who loveth not, nor hateth not; who neither rejoiceth nor findeth fault with world happenings; who grieveth not nor coveteth; who hath renounced both good and evil for sake of Me.

"And dear to Me, also, is he who regardeth equally both friend and foe; who sees repute and disrepute as one to the wise mind; who knows cold and heat, and pain and pleasure, to be not one more desirable than the other.

Such a one also regardeth not solicitously the passing of events; and to him praise and condemnation are the same. He is silent and well satisfied with whatsoever befall him or come to pass in the world; and he hath no particular place of abode in the world, but feeleth at home everywhere in Me. He, of whom I have just spoken, is of a steady and equable mind, and devotion is ever manifested by him —he verily loveth Me, and I him. He is very dear to Me.

"Yea, yea, they who imbibe this Water of Immortality—this Divine Nectar—of the teaching, as given by me to thee, O *Arjuna,* and receive it with faith and devotion, verily, are such dear and exceedingly beloved by Me."

THUS ENDETH PART XII OF THE BHAGAVAD GITA, WHICH PART IS CALLED THE "YOGA OF DEVOTION."

PART XIII.

THE KNOWER AND THE KNOWN.

Then spake *Arjuna* unto *Krishna,* the Blessed Lord, saying:

"Pray inform me, Blessed Lord, concerning that which we call the Personal Self, and that great Something beyond and above this, which we call the 'I,' or 'Ego,' or perchance, the 'Soul,' which knows. Tell me of this Knower and also of the Known, or which is seemingly Known."

KRISHNA: "That which thou calleth thy Personal Self, *Arjuna,* is called by philosophers, 'The Known.' That which thou calleth the 'I,' the 'Ego,' or the 'Soul,' is called by the philosophers 'the Knower.' And remember this, O Prince, that I am the Knower of the Known in whatever form it may appear and manifest. This understanding of the Knower and the Known is esteemed by Me as Wisdom worthy of attainment.

"Now, listen to My words, while I inform thee of the nature of the Known; what it resembleth; what are its various parts; from what it proceedeth; and also what is That which Knoweth the Known, and what are Its characteristics. Briefly will I state it—that which has been sung by the Sages in various chants; and which appeareth in manifold verses of the sacred writings, with many reasonings, arguments and proofs.

"The Personal Self is made up of the five *Mahabuta,* or Principles, known as follows, by the teachers: *Ahankara,* or the Consciousness of Personality; *Buddhi,* or Understanding or Intellect; *Avyaktam,* the unseen Vital Force; the eleven *Indriyas,* or sense-centers; and the five *Indriya-gochar,* or sense-organs; then cometh *Ichha* and *Dwesha,* or Love and Hatred; *Sukha and Dukha,* or Pleasure and Pain; *Chetana,* or Sensibility; and *Dhrita,* or Firmness. These, *Arjuna,* constitute the Personal Self—the Known—and its characteristics.

"Spiritual Wisdom consists in freedom from Self-esteem or Hypocrisy, or Injury to Others. It inculcates Patience; Rectitude; Respect for Teachers and Masters; Chastity; Steadfastness; Self-control; Freedom from

Sense-attachments; Freedom from Pride and Vainglory in the Personal Self; It brings a constant realization of the true nature of Birth and Death; Sickness and Decay; Pain and Imperfection. It also brings with it the loosening of the bonds of attachment in the personal relation between the possessor of Wisdom and his wife, children and home. It brings a constant equanimity and balance of mind and temper, notwithstanding the nature of the passing or occurring event, or whether it be desired or non-desirable.

"Such Wisdom also brings to its possessor a desire for unfailing and unrelaxing worship and devotion:—worship in private places and secluded spots; and a corresponding distaste for crowds of men. Likewise bringeth it a love of the Spirit which pervadeth all things; and the meditation upon the nature of Wisdom, and the goal awaiting its possessor, or traveller upon its path. This is what is called by philosophers, *Dnyana,* or Knowledge, as contrasted with *Adnyana,* or Ignorance.

"Now, will I inform thee what is called *Dneya,* or the Object of Wisdom, for the right knowledge and understanding of which thou shalt enjoy Immortality. This Object of Wisdom is that which the teachers and philosophers call *Brahma,* or Universal Life. The Universal Life hath no beginning, and can be called neither Being nor yet Non-Being. In the midst of the world it dwelleth, and envelopeth all the universe even to its utmost ends. In itself free from every organ and sense, yet doth it manifest through every organ and sense in all the universe. Unattached and free, it containeth all things within its nature—and free from qualities or attributes, yet doth it partake of the knowledge of all qualities and attributes. Within and yet without—inside and outside—it is. And inanimate and animate is it—movable and non-movable, in and throughout all Nature. It is infinite in its minuteness, and is therefore invisible and imperceptible. And yet although most near, yet it is also afar off. Undivided is it in its nature, and yet infinite in its apparent division.

"It is the womb of all things—from it proceedeth creation and destruction. It is the source of Light—beyond all darkness is it. It is Wisdom—also that which is the object of Wisdom—and also that which is to be obtained by Wisdom. In the minds and hearts of all, it dwelleth always.

"This then is what is known as *Kshetra* or the Personal Self; *Dnyna,* or Wisdom; and *Dneya,* or the Object of Wisdom. Thus hath been told thee the secret of the Substance of Life, and its distribution and moulding. The Wise One, thus knowing, entereth into Me.

"Know also, *Arjuna,* that *Prakriti,* or Nature, and also *Purusha,* the Soul, are both without beginning. Knoweth thou, also, O Prince, that the Principles of Nature are inherent in Nature, and from her they flow out. Nature is that which produceth what we call Cause and Effect, or Causation; it is the Source of Action.

"Knoweth thou also, Arjuna, that Soul, seated in Nature, or in Nature's Matter, receiveth the impressions which proceed from Material Life. It is the Principle which is operative in the experiences of Pleasure and Pain. The consequences of these impressions and experiences and the attachment thereto, on the part of the personal manifestation of Soul, is the cause of birth and rebirth. The incidents and circumstances of reincarnation

arise therefrom, and persist until the higher
Wisdom is gained, which overcometh the
qualities that bind the soul to the things and
objects of the material world. The Soul is
that superior nature of one, which, dwelling
in the body, doth observe, direct, protect and
partake of Life.

"He who thus comprehendeth *Prakriti,* or
Nature; *Purusha,* or Soul; and the *Gunas,* or
Principles of Nature, even as I have spoken
of them to thee, *Arjuna,* though he may be
living in any state or condition or manner—
he shall not be again subject to mortal birth.

"Some men, by means of meditation, behold
the Universal Soul within Nature—the Soul
within the Body. Others attain the perception
by means of Renunciation of Action. And
others, still, by the Service of Right Action.
Others there be who have not discovered this
truth of themselves, and in themselves; but
have heard the doctrine and teachings from
others, and thereafter heed the same and respect it and attend unto it. Yea, I say unto
you, O *Arjuna,* that even these last, if they
manifest earnest faith and attention, and observe the truth thus obtained by them—even

they shall lay the foundations of immortality, and pass beyond the Gulf of Death.

"Knoweth thou, O Prince of Pandu, that every thing that is created, be it animate or inanimate, is produced by the combination of Soul and Nature—the Knower and the Known. He who seeth the Universal Soul immanent in all things—imperishable, although in all perishable things—verily, indeed such a one truly seeth. Seeing the same Universal Soul immanent in all things, he avoideth the error of identifying the Self with the lower principles, and thus he is released from the illusion of mortality, and goes forward on the road to immortality.

"He who sees that his actions are really performed by Nature, and Nature's principles, and that the Soul is not to be entangled therein—he sees indeed. When he perceiveth that all the various forms of Nature's manifestations are really rooted in the One Life, and from thence are spread forth in their branches, limbs, twigs, and leaves of infinite variety—then he passeth into a consciousness of the One Life.

"The Spirit, O Prince—the Spirit of the

Universal Soul—even when it is within one of Nature's bodily forms, never really acts nor is really affected. Because of its essential nature, it is above and beyond action. And being without beginning, and without qualities or attributes, it is beyond the storm of action and change. The Universal Ether is not affected by the action of objects within it and within which it is. And even so is the Universal Soul, in which are all material forms, and which is within all material forms—so is it unaffected by the action and changes of those forms, although it knows them all, as the Knower of the Known.

"Even as doth the single Sun illuminate the whole world, O *Arjuna,* so doth the One Soul illumine the whole of Nature—the One Knower, the whole Field of the Known.

"And he who by the power of Spiritual Wisdom doth perceive this difference between the Soul and the Material and Personal Self; between the Soul and Nature and Nature's Principles—between the Knower and the Known—verily he perceiveth the liberation of the Soul from the illusion of Matter and Personality, and he passeth to the Spiritual Consciousness, in which all is seen as One Reality, without Illusion or Error."

THUS ENDETH PART XIII OF THE BHAGAVAD GITA, WHICH PART IS CALLED "THE KNOWER AND THE KNOWN."

PART XIV.

THE THREE GUNAS OR QUALITIES.

Then spake unto *Arjuna,* the Prince of the Pandus, *Krishna,* the Blessed Lord, saying:

"Draw near, *Arjuna,* and I will further inform you in the Supreme Wisdom—that Wisdom of all Wisdom the best—that Wisdom by which the Wise Ones mounted unto the heights of Supreme Attainment and perfection. And, such, having become blended into Me, by reason of this Wisdom, they are not again reborn, even in the creation of a new universe at the beginning of a Day of *Brahm,* nor are they blotted out upon the dissolution of the universe, at the beginning of a Night of *Brahm.*

"Know thou, *Arjuna,* that Nature is the Great Womb in which I place my seed—from this proceedeth all natural forms, shapes, things, and objects. Nature is the Great Womb of all those things which are conceived in the natural womb, and I am the Father whose Seed is within the seed of all natural things.

"The three great *Gunas,* or Principles of
Nature, oft times called the Three Qualities,
and which are inherent in, and which spring
from Nature, are known by these names, O
Prince; *Sattvas,* or Truth; *Rajas,* or Passion;
and *Tamas,* or Indifference—these be the
Three. And each, and all, tend to bind the
Soul within the Body—the Universal Soul
within Nature. As Above so Below, the
Three serve to bind and hold the higher to the
lower. But the binding differeth in its nature,
O Prince, though all are bonds. Thus *Sattvas,*
or Truth, being pure and stainless, bindeth the
sould by attachment to Wisdom and Harmony,
and bringeth it back to re-birth because of the
bonds of Knowledge and Understanding.
And, *Rajas,* or Passion, is of the nature of
burning Desire, and doth bind the soul by attachment to Action, and Things and Objects,
and doth bring it back to re-birth because of
the bonds of Worldly Hunger and Thirst for
Having and Doing. And *Tamas,* or Indifference, is of an ignorant, dark, stupid and heavy
nature, and bindeth the soul by attachment to
Sloth, and Idleness, and Folly and Indolence,
bringing it back to re-birth because of the

bonds of Ignorance, Stupidity, Heedlessness and Low-Content.

"To *Sattvas Guna,* pertaineth Wisdom and Harmony; to *Rajas Guna* pertaineth Action and Possessions; and to *Tamas Guna* pertaineth Sloth, Stupidity and Indolence. When one overcometh the *Tamas* and the *Rajas,* then the *Sattvas* reigneth. When the *Rajas* and *Sattvas* are overcome, then reigneth the *Tamas.* When the *Tamas* and *Sattvas* have been overcome, then reigneth the *Rajas.*

"When Wisdom is manifest in one, then know that the *Sattvas* is the ruling *Guna.* When great Action is manifest, or great Desire is apparent, then know you that *Rajas* is the *Guna* ruling. When Stupidity, Sloth, Idleness and Lack of Thought is manifest, then know thou truly that *Tamas Guna* is on the throne.

"When the soul forsakes the body in which the *Sattvas* ruleth, then does it proceed to the plane inhabited by the Wise and Intelligent. When it leaves the body in which the *Rajas* hath been the strongest, then doth it pass to the plane of rest, from whence in time it is reborn again in a body adapted to the manifestation of action, and possessed of a tendency toward Desires, and among people and enivronment adapted to and in harmony with these qualities. When it leaves the body in which the *Tamas* hath been in the ascendent, then doth it pass to re-birth in a body, and among those in harmony with its low plane of manifestation.

"The fruit of *Sattvas* is called good; the fruit of *Rajas* is called pain and dissatisfaction and unrest. The fruit of *Tamas* is called Ignorance and Stupidity and Inertia. From *Sattvas* is produced Wisdom; from *Rajas*, Unrest and Covetousness; from *Tamas*, Ignorance, Delusion and Foolishness, together with Sloth. Those of the *Sattvas Guna*, are raised up on high; those of the *Rajas Guna* reach no higher than the middle plane, which is the plane of Man's world activities and life; while those of the *Tamas Guna* are borne down by the heavy weight of their quality and sink down far below.

"Say I unto thee, O Prince, that those who see that the only agents of action are these very *Gunas*, the Principles of Nature—and also discover that there is a Being superior to them—know the true nature of the Soul and enter into Me.

"And when an embodied soul hath passed beyond these three Qualities, which are in the Nature of all embodiment—and hath learned of the consciousness beyond them—then is that soul delivered from the bonds, and is freed from Birth and Death; Old Age and Pain; and drinketh of the Nectar of Immortality."

ARJUNA: "What are the distinguishing characteristics of the man who hath passed beyond the Three *Gunas,* or Qualities? How acteth he? And by what means hath he overcome and passed beyond the Three?

KRISHNA: "Hearken to my words, O Prince! He doth not hate these qualities, Wisdom, Energy and Ignorance, when they come to him—nor yet longeth after them when they are not with him; but unattached to either like or dislike for them, he sitteth neutral among the coming and going thereof, unmoved and unshaken by them—knowing that the *Gunas,* or Qualities, exist and are constantly coming and going, yet witnessing their succession and movement as one outside who witnesseth a procession of objects.

"Yet, even he who standeth self-reliant, and at ease, balanced equally between pleasure and pain—he to whom a stone, iron, and gold seem alike and equally valuable—he who appeareth the same amidst like and dislike; and who regardeth praise and blame with equal emotion, or lack of emotion—he who is ever the same in honor or disgrace—he who knoweth no difference between treatment of friend or foe—he who hath forsaken all ambition for enterprises or undertakings of a worldly kind —verily hath such a one surpassed and passed beyond the effects of the Three *Gunas,* or Qualities, and escaped from them.

"And he, my follower and devotee, who hath devoted himself entirely to Me, and who serveth Me with exclusive heart and mind— he having completely passed beyond the qualities, is surely fitted to be blended with the One.

"Yea, verily, sayeth I unto thee, *Arjuna,* that I am the Symbol and the Reality of Immortality; the Eternal; the Absolute Justice; the Bliss Unending."

THUS ENDETH PART XIV OF THE BHAGAVAD GITA, WHICH PART IS CALLED "THE THREE GUNAS OR QUALITIES."

PART XV.

CONSCIOUSNESS OF THE SUPREME.

Once more, spake *Krishna,* the Blessed Lord, unto *Arjuna,* saying:

"The *Ashwattha,* the sacred tree, the symbol of the Universe in our teachings, is said to be indestructible. Its roots are above, and its branches are below. Its leaves are the *Vedas,* or Sacred Writings. He who knowest this, knowest the *Vedas.* Its branches grow out of the Three Qualities, or *Gunas;* and their lesser shoots or twigs are the organs of sense, some spreading forth high up, and others down low. The roots which are spreading abroad below, on the plane of men, are the bonds of action.

"Its form is beyond the knowledge of men; as is its beginning, its end, or its connections. When this mighty tree is finally cut down by the strong axe of Discriminative Non-Attachment, in spite of its strongly fixed roots—then the destroyer of that tree shalt seek for that place from which there is no more return to

re-birth, for that place is the One Supreme
Soul, from which floweth out the Soul immanent in and animating all things.

"There be those who, having freed themselves from pride, ignorance and delusion,
have overcome those faults which arise from
attachments to action. They employ their
minds constantly in contemplation of the Real
Self, and thus are restrained from inordinate
desires, and made free from attraction of the
Pairs of Opposites, and from the attendant effect of these which are known as Pleasure and
Pain. They are thus relieved of confusion
and illusion, and they ascend to that plane
which endureth forever. They pass on to that
place which is not lighted by either the sun or
the moon, nor yet by fire, but which is yet
radiant beyond imagination. For this place is
My Supreme Abode, and there is no return
therefrom.

"Yea, it is even a portion of myself, that, as
an apparently separate soul doth draw around
itself the five senses and the mind, that it may
obtain embodiment in a mortal frame and
that it may leave this frame again. And the
Ego carrieth this mind and these senses to

whatever body he inhabits, and again carrieth they away again when he leaves that body. Through the instrumentality of the organs of seeing, hearing, feeling, smelling and tasting, together with the mind, he experienceth the objects of sense.

"The deluded and ignorant do not see the soul when it leaves the body, or remaineth in the body; nor yet when as swayed by the *Gunas,* or Qualities, it experienceth the objects of sense. But the Wise Ones see and understand. And, there are those who, by industrious meditation, acquire an inward sight by which they may perceive this occurrence within themselves—but those of untrained minds and ignorant understanding, though laboring hard, yet fail to so perceive this within themselves.

"Know thou, *Arjuna,* that the light and radiance which proceedeth from the sun and enlighteneth and illumineth the whole world—and that radiance which proceedeth from the moon, and sheddeth soft beams over the earth—and the fiery flame within the fire, which burneth fiercely upon all upon which its light falleth—all this splendor is of Me.

"Know, also, O Prince, that I enter the earth and nourish all living things by my life and vitality. I am the life-giving juice of the plants and growing things. Likewise am I the Vital Force—the Fire of Life—which performeth the functions of life within the body —I inspire the breathing, and I direct the digestive, assimilative and eliminative processes. I am in the hearts and minds of men, and from Me proceedeth memory and knowledge and also the absence of both.

"And, all that is to be known from the *Vedas* am I. Yea, verily am I also the wisdom of the *Vedanta* and the knowledge of the *Vedas*.

"There are two aspects of Soul in this world—the One, and the Many—the Over-Soul and the Under-Souls—the Undivided and the Divided—many names there be to express this truth, and yet all names fail to express it fully. The Many-Soul is manifest in the body of Nature, and in the bodies of Nature's forms—the One-Soul standeth apart and above Nature, and Nature's things. And yet both of these are but aspects of One. Yea, and there is also the Spirit—the Soul of the

Soul—the Supreme—the Highest—the Sustainer—the Source—the Lord—yea, even I, *Krishna,* who, dwelling within and yet above the One-Soul and the Many-Soul, am SPIRIT ABSOLUTE.

"Verily, verily, I say unto you, *Arjuna,* and to all who follow after, that he whose eyes have been cleared of the Smoke of Illusion and who knoweth me, *Krishna,* thus as SPIRIT ABSOLUTE; and who thus knowing, loveth me with all his heart, and all his mind, and all his soul—he knoweth ME in truth. And knowing ME, he knoweth all things, and worshipeth and loveth the ONE and ALL.

"Now, *Arjuna,* have I declared unto thee the Secret of Secrets—the Mystery of Mysteries—which once fully understood and comprehended, O Prince, bringeth to one the Supreme Illumination. Who knoweth this hath done all that is to be done—he hath accomplished the Divine Adventure—he hath gained All that can be Known."

THUS ENDETH PART XV OF THE BHAGAVAD GITA, WHICH PART IS CALLED "CONSCIOUSNESS OF THE SUPREME."

PART XVI.

Now again, spake *Krishna,* the Blessed Lord, unto *Arjuna,* saying:

"These be the characteristics and nature of those who are walking The Path that leadeth to Heavenly Rewards—these are the marks of Good Character and Destiny. Fearlessness have they, and Purity of Heart. And a steady attention to the Life of Wisdom. And Charity; and Self-Mastery and True Religious Inclination; and Earnest Study; and Temperate Living. And Right Action; and Freedom from Evil Doing; and Truthfulness; and Fredom from Anger. And Renunciation; and Equanimity; and Freedom from Evil Speaking of others. Love and Compassion for all beings; Freedom from the Desire to Kill; Mildness; Modesty; Discretion; Dignity; Patience; Fortitude; Chastity; Forgiveness; and Freedom from Vainglory.

"And these be the characteristics and nature of those who are walking the downward path

that leadeth to Loss of Heavenly Rewards—
these are the marks of Evil Character and
Destiny. Hypocrisy is theirs, and Pride; and
Arrogance; and Conceit; and Anger; and
Harsh Speech; and Ignorance.

"Yea, the Good Character and Destiny
make for Liberation from Mortality, and for
the Absorption in the Divine. And the Evil
Character and Destiny make for repeated
birth and re-birth amidst the mire of Mortality. The one meaneth Freedom—the other
Bondage. Feareth not, *Arjuna,* for thou hast
the Good Character and Destiny, and Freedom
shall be thine.

"There are two kinds of Natures observable
among human beings in the world—the Good
Nature and the Evil Nature. The characteristics of the Good Nature have been spoken
of. Listeneth thou now, O *Arjuna,* to a re-
cital of the characteristics of the Evil Nature.

"Those who possess the Evil Nature, O
Prince, knoweth not what it is to perform
Right Action, and to refrain from performing
Wrong Action. Nor is Purity, Morality or
Veracity to be found in them. They lack
Faith and in their folly would believe that

the universe hath no creator, but is in itself without beginning or end, and is its own cause. They deny the existence of Law or Truth in the universe. And they deny the existence of Spirit. They believe in Materialism, in Godlessness, and they hold that Lust is the moving and operating cause of all things, bringing about mutual union and reproduction.

"And, believing these evil and foolish things, these men of imperfect understanding, with this conception fixed in their minds, devote themselves to evil deeds and sow in the world the seeds of Evil Thought and Error. They live for Carnal Enjoyment, teaching this as the highest good. They strive after gratification of sensual appetites, and the creation of new appetites—and there is no peace or satisfaction in them, for appetite springeth from appetite, and the sensual craving groweth more acute in the measure in which it is gratified. Such men are hypocrites, and full of madness and intoxication.

"Because of their folly and false reasoning, they invent new doctrines and theories, and give themselves to the material life of sensual enjoyment.   They live and die in their delusions, holding to the error that in the gratification of the sensual nature alone is satisfaction and happiness to be found.   Believing that death endeth all for them, they would fill their days of life full to the brim with sense gratification and the performance of the behests of an abnormal and perverted sensuality.   Desire is their God, and its worship and service their only religion.

"Bound by the thousand ties of Desire for Things and Objects, they are attached to the body of Lust and Wrath and Avarice.   They prostitute their minds and their sense of justice, in their vain search for wealth wherewith to gratify their inordinate and swollen appetite for sense experiences.

"They say unto themselves: 'To-day have I acquired this thing.   Tomorrow shall I acquire the desire of my heart.   This wealth have I gained, and tomorrow shall I gain that other wealth also.   This foe hath been slain, and tomorrow others shall I destroy.   I am my own God—there is none other God but Me—and I shalt enjoy this my world, which is mine for the pleasure I may extract from it.

I am rich and overflowing with wealth. I take precedence among other men. Where is there one alike so perfect, wise, and shrewd as I? I will scatter handfuls of money among the throng, that they may realize my bounty, and know how great, powerful and rich am I— yea, even I.' In this manner do these fools talk—they who imagine themselves wise, but who in reality have disordered and unbalanced minds.

"And such, confounded and confused in their minds by reason of their delusions, excesses, and vain living—they become entangled in the nets of their own desires and attachments. And the weight of their objects of attachment, holding them fast, drags them down into the quicksands of Hell, which is the repeated re-birth into the lower and lower planes of the mire and slime of Maternality and Sensuality. There is no Hell like unto this, even among the imaginings of those who would teach of places of torment and torture—this is the most fearful Hell of all.

"Yea, and some of these men, in their hy-pocrisy and desire to appear well before the world, do even ape piety and true religion.

Following the letter instead of the spirit, they imitate the worship, and perform the churchly rites and ceremonies, with much show of zeal; with much outward show and display; and with ostentatious scattering of alms. Their Ignorance, and Conceit, and Self-esteem follow them into the temple, and they pollute the holy places with their thievish presence and natures.

"Being filled with Pride, Power, Ostentation, Lust and Selfishness, they are consumed with Hate, Malice and Slander, and hate Me in themselves and in others. Wherefore, are these vile, sensual, hating, pitiless ones—these evil beings who hate Me and all that is Good —cast down into continual re-birth into the wombs of mire and filth and uncleanliness.

"And, if even in these lower depths of uncleanliness, they learn not the lesson, and grow not sick and filled with nausea at the filth of sensuality and long not to begin the upward path from the Hell into which they have been cast—if they learn not even this lesson, but, instead, still true to their nature, they prefer to sink to lower and still lower planes—then finally they sink into the final stage which

meaneth Annihilation.   And thus do they lose
their souls indeed and exist no more, even as
their foolish philosophies have taught them to
expect, but in a far different manner and
even from causes which they strenuously denied.   Such come not to Me—ever or at any
time—but are lost forever and ever, for from
Nothingness there is no return.

"Three passages are there to this Hell of
Lower Re-birth, and these three are, Lust,
Anger and Avarice—the destroyers of the
soul if finally persisted in.   Therefore should
men avoid them as demoniac roads to destruction and Inferno.   He who renounceth them
as such, and freeing himself from the *Tamas
Guna,* or Dark Quality, shall rise upward, and
advancing step by step, shall regain The Path
which leadeth to the Heavenly State of the
Divine Union.   But he who abandoneth the
dictates of Spiritual Wisdom, and giveth himself up to the delusions and errors of Lust,
Anger and Avarice, verily shalt he attain
neither Perfection, Happiness, nor the Divine
State.

"Wherefore, O *Arjuna,* thou should acquaint thyself with the highest Spiritual

Teachings; and the understanding regarding Right Action and Wrong Action, that thou may perform the one and avoid the other. Seeketh thou the Highest Light of Wisdom, and govern thy works accordingly."

THUS ENDETH PART XVI, OF THE BHAGAVAD GITA, WHICH PART IS CALLED "THE GOOD AND EVIL NATURES."

PART XVII.

Thus further, spake *Arjuna*, unto *Krishna*, the Blessed Lord, saying:

"What is the condition and state of those men who casteth aside the authority of the Sacred Writings, yet who still retain their faith and worship? Are they under the control of the *Sattvas;* the *Rajas;* or the *Tamas Gunas?* Tell me thus, O Blessed *Krishna*, my Lord, I pray Thee!"

KRISHNA: "The Faith of Man is of a threefold kind—three forms of manifestations hath it, according to the nature, character and disposition of the man. Named after the *Gunas* are these three forms, namely *Sattvakee; Rajasee;* and *Tamasee*—or in other words, The Pure; the Desire-colored; and The Dark. Heareth thou what these are, O Prince.

"The faith of each man is a reflection of that man's character or nature. That in which each hath faith, is the essence of that man himself. Each man's God—his Conception of

Deity—is himself at his best, magnified to infinity. Likewise, is his Evil Spirit, or Devil, but himself at his worst, magnified to infinity. By one's Dieties shalt thou know the man himself, if thou observest well.

"This being so, those in whom the *Sattvas Guna* is supreme, worshippeth the Gods—the most advanced worshipping only the Absolute Spirit—ME! And those under the mastery of the *Rajas Guna*, worshippeth the lesser gods —the gods of qualities, attributes, powers, gifts; or other exalted beings of the higher planes and regions. And those under the dominion of the dark *Tamas Guna*, worship the departed spirits, ghosts, goblins, devils, demons, gnomes, evil spirits and the elementals, and such beings of the lower planes of the unseen world, oftimes times calling them by the name of God.

"As for those misguided men, who seek merit by the performance of severe austerities, and mortifications of the flesh, unauthorized by the Sacred Teachings—they are gainglorious creatures, overcome with pride, self-righteousness and hypocrisy, and are urged on by desire and passion for reward and praise.

These men torture the fair body, and torment the parts and principles of the same—thus disturbing the soul which resideth within, and even Me who am within the soul in its inner chamber. Such are demoniacal, in their infernal resolves and wrongful practices.

"Know thus also, *Arjuna,* that there be three kinds of food which are dear to all mankind. Also are Worship, Zeal, and Charity threefold. Hearken thou to their distinctions.

"The food that is most agreeable to those in whom the *Sattvas Guna* is predominant, is that conducive to Long Life, Power and Strength, and which prevents Sickness, and renders one Happy and Contented. Such food is pleasing to the taste; nourishing, substantial, and gratifying to the hunger. Too bitter it is not; neither is it too sour, too salt, too hot, too pungent, too astringent, nor too burning. Those of the *Rajas Guna* nature, prefer food which is bitter, sour, hot, pungent, dry and burning, to an excessive degree— that which stirs up the appetites, stimulates the taste-sense and produces, finally, pain, sickness, and dissatisfaction. Those who are under the rule of the dark *Tamas Guna,* in·

cline to food which hath been dressed the day
before, and that which is out of season; also
that which hath lost its savor and hath grown
putrid; also the uneaten parts of others' meals,
and all food that is unclean and impure.

"And as to Worship, know the three forms.
The man of *Sattvas Guna* doth worship according to the custom of the Sacred Writings
without desire of reward; with pure heart
worship for the love of worship; and with a
mind ever attentive to that which he worshippeth. And he, of the *Rajas Guna* nature, doth
worship as the hypocrite with mind full of
hope of reward; asking favors and seeking
merit and notice—such is his vain worship.
And he of the *Tamas Guna* nature doth worship without faith, or devotion, or thought,
or reverence, and without spirit—such is his
so-called worship, which is not worship at all,
but which is merely a form of habit and custom, and stupid, sheep-like following of cus-
tomary motions and forms.

"Respect for the Heavenly Beings; the
Holy Men; the Learned Men; Masters; together with Chastity, Rectitude, the Worship
of God, and Harmlessness—these constitute

what is known as Bodily Zeal. Gentleness, Justice, Kindness, Soft Speech, and Performance of Duty—these are what is known as the Zeal of Speech. Mental Content; Mildness of Temper; Devotion; Control over Passions; Purity of Soul—these are what are known as Mental Zeal.

"This Threefold zeal, which is performed by men who longeth not for reward or fruit of action, but who are stirred and warmed by True Faith—this belongeth to the *Sattvas Guna*. But the Zeal which springeth from hypocrisy and is built upon hope of reward; the reputation of piety and sanctity; honor and good-name; that which is uncertain and not constant—that belongeth to *Rajas Guna.* And the Zeal which is manifested by the foolish and stupid, and which consisteth of self-torture and similar folly, or which is performed in the hopes of injuring or destroying another—that belongeth to *Tamas Guna.*

"And as for Charity, these are the three kinds. That Charity which is bestowed for Charity's sake and because it is right; disinterestedly, and at due time, place and season, and to proper objects—this is of the *Satt-*

vas Guna. And that Charity which is be-stowed in expectation or hope of return, or reward; or attached to the fruits of action, or begrudgingly—this is of *Rajas Guna.* And that Charity which is bestowed out of place and season to unworthy objects; ungraciously and scornfully, the real spirit of Charity being entirely absent from the gift—this is of the *Tamas Guna.*

"'AUM—TAT—SAT,' this is the Three-fold Designation of the ABSOLUTE. By the Absolute, in the beginning were appointed the Teachers; the Sacred Teachings; and Re-ligion. Hence before the ceremonies, sacri-fices, rites, and religious teachings, cometh the pronouncing of the Sacred Syllable, 'AUM.' And before the performance of the rites of sacrifice and the ceremonies, almsgiving, aus-terities, zeal and worship, of those who seek Immortality, comes the pronouncing of the word 'TAT.' And in the state of mental wor-ship, sacrifice, and renunciation, when action is at rest—also in the performance of good actions, and in the observance of good quali-ties—also in the dedication of action and life to the Supreme—then is pronounced the word 'SAT.'

"And whatever is performed without Faith whether it be sacrifice; charity; mortifications of the flesh; austerity; or any other act or observance which lacketh goodness, truth and faith—that is called 'ASAT,' and is without merit of virtue, either in this world or in other worlds; either here or hereafter."

THUS ENDETH PART XVII OF THE BHAGAVAD GITA, WHICH IS CALLED "THE THREEFOLD FAITH."

PART XVIII.

Then spake *Arjuna,* unto *Krishna,* the Blessed Lord, saying:

"O Blessed Lord, inform me, I pray thee, regarding the nature of *Sannyasa,* or the Abstaining from Action, on the one hand; and *Tyaga,* or the Renunciation of the Fruits of Action, on the other hand. Pray tell me, O Lord, of the true principle of each and also of the differences and distinction between these two.

KRISHNA: "The Sages have told us that the principle of *Sannyasa,* or Abstaining from Action, lieth in the forsaking of all Action which hath a desired object; and that the principle of *Tyaga,* or Renunciation of Fruits of Action, lieth in the forsaking of all the Fruits of every Action. Notest thou this subtle distinction, O Prince? Then, also, have certain teachers informed us that Actions are to be forsaken as evil, yea, even as evil as crimes. Still other teachers have informed us

164

that actions of worship, sacrifice, austerity, and devotion, are worthy and virtuous, and therefore should not be forsaken. In view of this confusion of teachings, hear thou, O Prince, to this my certain teaching upon this subject of *Tyaga,* or the Renunciation of the Fruits of Action, which is taught as being threefold.

"Tyaga, or Renunciation of Action, doth not rest in the forsaking of virtuous and religious action. Therefore actions of worship, devotion, austerity, and charity, are not to be forsaken or renounced. For most proper are they. Performance, and devotion, austerity, and charity are the purifiers of the teachers and philosophers.

"It is my certain teaching, O Arjuna, that such virtuous and religious actions and works are to be performed for their own sake—for their own inherent virtue—and not from hope of reward here or hereafter, but with full renunciation of reward, merit, consequences or fruits of the action or works. The teaching that it is proper to abstain from these virtuous works, (which surely are to be performed by the virtuous), is erroneous, **false**

and improper—and the following of such per-
nicious teachings result from the folly and
confusion of mind resulting from the *Tamas
Guna,* or Quality of Ignorance.

"And also know this, O Prince, that most
erroneous is the forsaking of work and action,
for the reason that it is painful, tiresome and
unpleasant to the physical body, or because it
is unattractive to the mind. Verily he that
for these reasons leaveth undone that which
he should have done, and would take merit
therefor, he is self-deceived and shall not obtain the merit accruing from Renunciation.
This folly doth arise from the *Rajas Guna,* or
Quality of Desire.

"But that work and action which is performed because it seemeth proper and necessary to be done, providing it be performed
with a full forsaking of the consequences and
fruits, and without hope or expectation of
reward, verily such is true Renunciation,
most proper, good and pure. Such ariseth
from *Sattvas Guna,* or the Quality of Truth
and Intelligence.

"And, he who is moved by the *Sattvas
Guna,* or Quality of Truth and Intelligence,

verily, is known as a *Tyagee,* or a Renouncer
of the Fruit of Action. His judgment is most
sound, and he has risen above doubt and distraction of mind. He rejoiceth not in the attainment of successful results, neither doth he
complain over the failure of his actions—he
accepteth either, being attached to neither.

"Know thou, Arjuna, that it were the
veriest folly to attempt to absolutely abstain
from action and works—the very constitution
of the mortal body forbiddeth it. Therefore, he is most properly called a *Tyagee* who
is a Renouncer of the Fruit of Action. The
Fruit of Action is threefold, namely: that
which is coveted or desired; that which is de-
tested and undesired; and that which is neither
one or the other, being of mixed quality and
undetermined nature. And these fruits, according to their nature, accrue after death
and in re-birth, to those who earn them. But
where there is no seed of Fruit in the Action,
there is no fruit. And where the Fruits are
renounced, none accrueth.

"Learn from Me, Arjuna, that for the performance of every act five agents are necessary, as is declared in the Sacred Teachings.

These are the body; the acting mind; the various energies; the muscles and nerves; and the soul. All work or actions which engageth a man—the work of the body, or work of the mind, or speech, whether good or evil, lawful or unlawful, hath these five agents in operation in the performance. He therefore, who knoweth this, and yet conceiveth the Real Self to be the sole agent of the action is as one blind, and seeth not in truth. He who hath freed himself from the bonds of Personality, and who hath gained Right Understanding, verily he knoweth that although he destroyeth these hosts gathered together in battle-array, yet hath he killed not at all, nor is he bound by the Fruit of his Action in his re-births.

"There be Three Moving Causes of Action —those which precede the performance of every act—they are *Dyana* or Knowledge; *Dyena,* or the Object of Knowledge; and *Parijnata,* or the Knower. Thus the Knowledge, the Known, and the Knower—these be the three Moving Causes of Action. Likewise is the accomplishment of an action, threefold, namely: The Implement; the Act; and the Agent.

"Knoweth thou, also, that the Wisdom, the Action, and the Agent, hath each its distinguishing characteristics, produced by the influence of the Three *Gunas,* or Qualities. Learn now, the influence of the Qualities, or *Gunas,* as manifested therein.

"That *Dnyana,* or Wisdom, which is of the *Sattvas Guna,* or Quality of Truth, is that by which a man believeth and understandeth that One Principle—indestructible and eternal, and not separated—prevaileth and manifesteth in all Nature, in all of her destructible and separated forms. And that *Dnyana,* or Wisdom, which is of the *Rajas Guna,* or Quality of Desire and Passion, is that by which a man believeth and understandeth that in Nature there are manifold Principles prevailing, instead of One. And that *Dynana,* or Wisdom, which is of the *Tamas Guna,* or Quality of Ignorance and Stupidity, is that by which a man believeth and understandeth not any Principle whatsoever; and which looking not beyond the form, nor beneath the surface of things, seeth each object or thing, regard-

less of its relation to another or to the whole
—thinking of each as if it were the whole—
without any conception of Cause or Origin—
bathed in Slothful Thought and Ignorance.

"That Act which one performeth as lawful
and virtuous, without regard for its consequences, fruit, or reward—dispassionately and
without attachment—that proceedeth from
the *Sattvas Guna*. And that Act which one
performeth with great care and concern for
consequences, and rewards—inspired by selfish desire and egotism—that proceedeth from
the *Rajas Guna*. And that Act which one performeth regardless whether it be Right Action or Wrong Action—heedless of its possible
evil and hurtful effects upon others—that
which is performed in ignorance, stupidity or
folly—that proceedeth from the *Tamas Guna*.

"That Agent, who is free from selfishness
and personal pride—who hath fortitude and
resolution—and who regardeth not the fruit
of his right action, neither looketh for reward
—he is moved by the *Sattvas Guna*. And that
Agent who is filled with desire, passion, and
hope of selfish gain and reward—who is avaricious, lacking in sympathy, impure, and a

bondsman of joy or sorrow—he is moved by the *Rajas Guna*. And that Agent, who is stupid, slothful, inattentive, stubborn, indiscreet, careless, inactive, and dilatory, and who lacketh energy and the right spirit of work— he is moved by the *Tamas Guna*.

"And, further, O *Arjuna*, Prince of Pandu, who art my pupil and dearly beloved student, listen while I inform thee clearly and without reserve concerning the threefold divisions and nature of Intelligence and Will.

"That Intelligence which knoweth how and when to enter into an undertaking, and how and when to withdraw; what is needful to be done, and what is needful to refrain from doing;—which knoweth what is Fear, what Fearlessness, and what Prudent Caution; what is Freedom, what Bondage, and what Foolish License;—that Intelligence cometh through *Sattvas Guna*. And that Intelligence which knoweth not fully what is proper and what is improper—what is right and what is wrong— this imperfect understanding being because of the sway of personal desire and passion, which warpeth the reason, and which causeth one to see every act by the light of his own personal desire—that Intelligence cometh through *Rajas Guna*. And that Intelligence which, wrapped in its dense stupidity and sloth, mistaketh Wrong for Right, Injustice for Justice and which seeth all things awry, distorted and inverted, and contrary to their real meaning and nature—that Intelligence cometh through *Tamas Guna.*

"That Will by which a man mastereth and controlleth himself, his mind, his actions, his organs, his body, with devotion and firmness —that Will ariseth from *Sattvas Guna.* And that Will by which a man is firm and persistent in his calling, from selfish desires and hope of reward; and which is employed in the furthering of avaricious undertakings; or in the gratification of lust—that Will ariseth from *Rajas Guna.* And that Will by which a man manifesteth a stubborn mind, like unto that of the wild ass, by which he holdeth fast to folly, ignorance, sloth, superstition, bigotry, foolish vanity, laziness, and fears—that Will ariseth from *Tamas Guna.*

"And, now, O Prince, hearken unto Me, while I inform thee regarding the threefold division of Pleasure, wherein Happiness conquereth Pain.

"The Pleasure that proceedeth from *Sattvas Guna,* is that which a man acquireth through his work and rightful energies—such is as poison at the beginning, and as nectar of sweetest flavor at the ending—this is the Pleasure of Right Attainment, which flows from Work Well-done—this is possible only to him of pure understanding and clear mind. The Pleasure that floweth from *Rajas Guna,* is that which a man experienceth through the union of the senses with the objects of their desire—such is as nectar in the beginning, but as bitter as poison in the ending—this belongeth to the nature of passion and desire. The Pleasure that proceedeth from *Tamas Guna,* is that which a man acquireth through idleness, indolence, drowsiness, the taking of drugs, and intoxication—such is as poison, both in the beginning and in the ending—this belongeth to the nature of darkness, sloth, and stupidity.

"Yea, the manifestation of the three *Gunas,* or Qualities is to be found everywhere in the earth and in regions above the earth—there is no creature or created thing on earth or in the super-terrestrial hosts, which is free from the operation of the *Gunas* or Qualities that spring from Nature's bosom.

"The duties of the various castes, and classes, and divisions of kind among men, are determined by these *Gunas* or Qualities, which are within the nature of each. The Priestly Caste of *Brahmans,* hath the duty of serenity, self-mastery, zeal, purity, patience, rectitude, wisdom, learning, and religious knowledge. The Warrior Caste, of *Kshatriyas*, hath the duty of courage, bravery, fortitude, honor, obedience, discipline, nobility and soldierly conduct. The Farmer Caste, of *Vaishyas,* hath the duty of industry, knowledge of the soil, of grains, of fruits, of cattle, and knowledge of trading, buying and selling. The Laboring Caste, of *Sudras,* hath the duty of faithful service, industry, attention, faithfulness, and honesty. And each duty is inspired and fostered by the Natural Disposition of each, which springeth from the *Gunas,* or Qualities, coming down to the man through his past thoughts, desires, and lives in the shape of character.

"Blessed is he that doeth his work as well as he can—that performeth his duty faithfully, according to his nature and walk of life—for from such good work coupled with a contented mind, doth Perfection arise.

"Listen thou, Arjuna, while I informeth thee how Perfection is gained by him who is intent upon his own duty, and who is faithful in the performance thereof.

"He who worketh to his best, in the line of his duty, and then offereth his work, and labor, and Duty, as a sacrifice to THE ABSOLUTE SPIRIT, from which proceedeth all the principles of Nature, Life, and the Universe, and from which is spread out the Universal Life in all of its forms and shapes and degrees of manifestation—he that worketh and who performeth his Duty in that spirit, verily I say unto thee, that man obtaineth Perfection by reason of such service and sacrifice. This is the Supreme Sacrifice of Life, which each man must offer to the Supreme Source of Life.

"Far better it is for one to perform his own Duty in the world, even though that work be lowly, and possessing faults, than the Duty of another, though the work be great and well;

performed. He who doeth the Duty and work established and indicated by his own nature, and character, erreth not. He who follows Nature's guidance in this, doeth well. Natural inclination toward occupation and manner of life, when coupled with ability for its performance, is worthy of performance, and thus becometh Duty. And then. let all remember, that every calling, or occupation, or duty, or manner or class of life, hath its painful side and its drawbacks and hindrances. Let all remember that every fire hath its smoke, and that it is folly to vainly imagine that one's own task is the hardest, and that the tasks of others are free from defects and hardships.

"One who hath a mind unattached, and unaffected by the pairs of opposites—whose mind is controlled, and whose Personal Self is mastered—whose desires are dead—he hath by Renunciation acquired the Highest Perfection of Freedom. He hath gained Freedom from Work, by the performance of Work without Desire for Fruits. Listen, now, while I inform thou how such an one, having gained this Perfection, may enter into the Eternal Bliss.

Having purified his mind, and cleared his understanding; having mastered his personal self by firm resolution, and having forsaken the objects of sense; having delivered himself from desire, dislike, and passion; worshipping with intelligent discretion and understanding; eating with moderation and temperance; with controlled speech, body and mind; being well practiced in meditation and concentration; being dispassionate; having freed himself from ostentation, egotism, tyranny, vain-glory, lust, anger, avarice, covetousness, and selfishness—possessing calmness and peace, amidst the feverish unrest of the world around him—such a man is fitted to enter into the consciousness of the Universal Life.

"And, having thus entered into this Universal Life Consciousness, he obtaineth absolute peace of mind, and he no longer wondereth, longeth, nor lamenteth. The same to all beings and things—and all beings and things the same to him—he attaineth Supreme Devotion to ME. And by this devotion to Me, gaineth he the fundamental knowledge of what I AM in ESSENCE. And having known what is

MY ESSENCE, he entereth, without hindrance or further obstacle, into MY BEING.

"Know, also, O Prince, that a man being engaged in any or every work—performing any or all actions—with faith, and devotion, and confidence in Me—placing his faith, and hope and confidence and mind upon Me and Me alone—he shall find his way to Me, and I to him. Then, O *Arjuna*, Well-Beloved, place thou thy heart, and soul and mind upon Me. Perform all thy acts, and work, and duty, for Me—place upon Me each and every one of them. Make me thy supreme choice and preference; and with the light of thine unfolded understanding, do thou think earnestly and constantly of Me. And by so doing, shalt thou, through my Divine Love, surmount and conquer every difficulty which doth surround and encompass all mortals.

"But, beware, lest in the pride of Personality thou heedst not My words and teachings, for if thou so failst in thy understanding and discrimination, then shalt thou escape Me, and I thee.

"And, if in thy self-sufficiency and half-wisdom, thou shouldst affirm to thyself: 'I

will not fight,' then shalt even that, thy determination, prove vain and fallacious—for even
then shalt the principle, qualities and character
of thy nature force thee into the fight, and
cause thee to grapple with thy foemen. Yea,,O
Prince, even that which thou, in thy illusion
and personal conceit, thinkst thou wilt not do,
even that shalt thy character, nature and qualities compel thee to do—from Duty there is no
escape—helpless art thou within the net. Being bound to thy *Dharma,* or Duty, by thy
Karma, or the Law of Cause and Effect, coming to thee from thy past lives, and the essence of which is thy nature and character,
with its qualities and tendencies—even so art
thou free only in one direction, and that is the
direction of thy Natural Duty, even that which
thou seekst in thy ignorance to avoid.

"Knoweth thou, Arjuna, that within the
heart of every being there dwelleth *Ishwara*—
the Master—who causeth all things to revolve
upon the wheels of Time. He is the Potter,
upon whose wheel these forms and shapes revolve, feeling the touch of his finger as he
moulds them into shape. Take refuge in Him,
and Him alone, O *Arjuna,* upon each and

every occasion of thy life; in all thine actions
and undertakings—for in him alone shalt thou
find Peace and Happiness, and a Safe Abode,
which endureth forever and forever. And in
this teaching of the truth, have I made known
to thee a knowledge which is a mystery of
Mystery—a secret of Secrets—a truth of
Truths. Ponder well upon it, O Prince, and
when thou fully understandst it, then act as
seemeth best unto thee, in the light of thy il-
luminated understanding.

"And now, O Prince of Pandu—*Arjuna*
my Well-Beloved Student—listen unto my
further and supremely mysterious teachings,
which now I shalt reveal unto thee, for thy
good, and because of my love for thee. Give
unto Me thy heart, and mind and soul, and
understanding, and thought, and interest and
attention, O *Arjuna,* My Beloved. Place them
all upon Me, who hath declared My true being unto thee. Serve Me alone; worship only
Me; bow down to Me alone; and I pledge thee
that thou shalt surely come to Me, thou who
art my loved one.

"Forsaking every other teaching, philosophy, science, or religion, fly to Me alone.

Grieve and distress thyself no longer, O *Arjuna,* for I shall surely deliver thee from all thy sins transgressions and short-comings.

"And, now a final word of caution to thee, *Arjuna*—hearken thou, and those who come after thee, to it, and govern ourselves accordingly. Know thou that this my teachings is not to be revealed to any who hath not subdued their bodies by devotion, or who are not my servants ; nor to those who are not willing and desirous to acquire the wisdom-teaching : nor to those who despise Me.

"They who shalt teach this divine wisdom —this supreme mystery—to those who are my servants ; and who practicing true devotion to Me, doth instruct them in My service; they shalt truly come unto Me. And, heed by words, *Arjuna*, there shall not be any among mankind who doth Me a greater kindness than this teaching and spreading of the Truth—nor shall there be any more dear to me than these.

"And, among those who shall come after thee, in all the long ages until the Night of Brahm shall have swept away all forms—if there be any among them who shall read, and hear, and study these teachings which I this day made known unto thee, as well as the words thou hast said unto me and to which I made reply—such shall do well, for verily shall I consider that by thus doing they have worshipped me, and such worship will I accept as a sacrifice. And the devotion of their minds shall rise unto Me. This is my promise.

"And even the man who shall listen to these teachings, in faith, and without reviling, shall also have his feet directed toward The Path which leadeth toward Happiness, and Peace, and during his periods of rest shall he be accorded admission to the regions wherein dwell those who have performed Right Action and Good Deeds.

"Hast thou heard and memorized these words which I have spoken unto thee, *Arjuna?* Hast thou listened with mind one-pointed and fixed upon Me? What hath become of the confusion and distraction of thought, which arose from thy ignorance and illusion, O Prince?"

ARJUNA: "By Thy Divine Power, O Immutable One, my Blessed Lord and Master, my mind hath been cleared of its confusion, and I see now with clear understanding, and

by the Light of the Spirit. I now stand firmly
fixed upon principles, and my doubts have
vanished into air. From this time on, shall I
act according to the Light of Thy Teachings.
In the Radiance of Thy Wisdom, so will I
Act!"

And then in conclusion spake *Sanjaya*, to
Dhritarashtra, the blind *Kuru* king, to whom
he had related this wondrous story of the
dialogue, between *Arjuna*, the Prince of the
Pandus, and *Krishna*, the Blessed Lord, and
visible manifestation in personal form of the
Absolute Spirit, saying:

"And now thou hast heard, O *Dhritarashtra*, of the wondrous words which I, even I
myself, overheard in this conversation between *Krishna* and *Arjuna*. By the favor of
some high being was I enabled to hear and
remember this mystic and wondrous doctrine
and teaching, as it fell from the lips of
Krishna himself. Remembering, again and
again, this holy conversation, am I filled with
great joy and happiness. And when I recall
the mysterious form of *Krishna*, My Lord,
then am I still more astonished, and still more
rejoiced. Wherever these words of *Krishna*,

the Lord, and *Arjuna*, the Prince, may chance to be seen, and read, and known—then even there too must come Prosperity, Attainment, and Happiness—yea Blessing and Peace. Of this I have no doubt—this is my belief."

THUS ENDETH PART XVIII OF THE BHAGAVAD GITA, WHICH IS CALLED "RENUNCIATION AND FREEDOM."

AND THUS COMETH TO AN END THE BHAGA-VAD GITA, OR THE MESSAGE OF THE MASTER, WHICH, WHEN TRULY UNDERSTOOD, WILL BRING TO ALL WHO READ IT, OR WHO HEAR IT, PEACE AND THE INNER WISDOM.

PEACE BE WITH YOU ALL!

"AUM"

The Complete Works
of
YOGI RAMACHARAKA

SCIENCE OF BREATH

FOURTEEN LESSONS—YOGI PHILOSOPHY

ADVANCED COURSE IN YOGI PHILOSOPHY

RAJA YOGA

GNANI YOGA

PHILOSOPHIES AND RELIGIONS OF INDIA

HATHA YOGA

PSYCHIC HEALING

MYSTIC CHRISTIANITY

LIFE BEYOND DEATH

BHAGAVAD GITA

THE SPIRIT OF THE UPANISHADS

PRACTICAL WATER CURE